The Heritage Trail

Tom Schofield

Published by Sigma Leisure – an imprint of
Sigma Press, Stobart House, Pontyclerc, Penybanc Road
Ammanford, Carmarthenshire SA18 3HP
This edition has been completely revised and updated with new maps and photographs

British Library Cataloguing in Publication Data

A CIP record for this book is available from the British Library

ISBN: 978-1-85058-857-3

Typesetting and Design by: Sigma Press, Ammanford, Carms

Maps and illustrations: Tom Schofield

Cover photograph: Lancashire and Yorkshire Railways Class 25, No. 957, leaving Mytholmes tunnel on the Keighley/Worth Valley Railway – Walk 10 (taken by Diane Schofield)

Printed by: Cromwell Press Group, Trowbridge, Wiltshire

Disclaimer: The information in this book is given in good faith and is believed to be correct at the time of publication. Care should always be taken when walking in hill country. Where appropriate, attention has been drawn to matters of safety. The author and publisher cannot take responsibility for any accidents or injury incurred whilst following these walks. Only you can judge your own fitness, competence and experience. Do not rely solely on sketch maps for navigation: we strongly recommend the use of appropriate Ordnance Survey (or equivalent) maps.

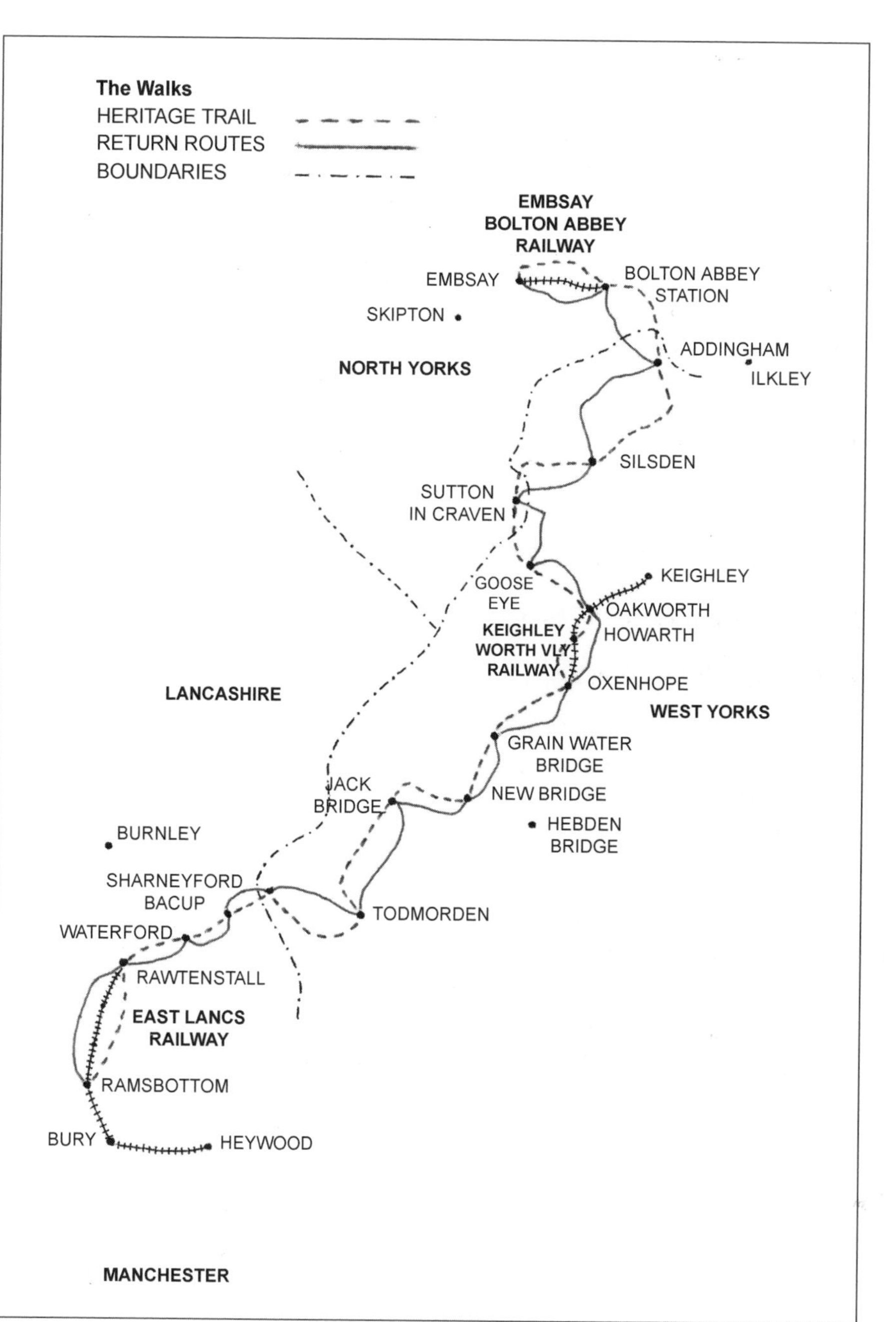
The Walks
HERITAGE TRAIL
RETURN ROUTES
BOUNDARIES
EMBSAY
BOLTON ABBEY
RAILWAY
EMBSAY
BOLTON ABBEY
STATION
SKIPTON
ADDINGHAM
ILKLEY
NORTH YORKS
SILSDEN
SUTTON
IN CRAVEN
GOOSE
EYE
KEIGHLEY
OAKWORTH
HOWARTH
KEIGHLEY
WORTH VLY
RAILWAY
OXENHOPE
LANCASHIRE
WEST YORKS
GRAIN WATER
BRIDGE
JACK
BRIDGE
NEW BRIDGE
HEBDEN
BRIDGE
BURNLEY
SHARNEYFORD
BACUP
TODMORDEN
WATERFORD
RAWTENSTALL
EAST LANCS
RAILWAY
RAMSBOTTOM
BURY
HEYWOOD
MANCHESTER

Legend

Public road	
Public road used on walk	
Footpath used on walk	
Return routes	
Unfenced road or track	
Buildings	
Church	+
Post Office	PO
Railway	
Railway (disused)	
Wall/hedge/fence	
Embankment/dyke	
Footbridge	FB
Gate	G
Stile	S
Stream/river	
Toilet	WC
Hillside	
Distance from Ramsbottom	20
Trees	
Resevoirs	
Car park	CP

Contents

Bolton Abbey Priory

Introduction

The Heritage Trail is a 54 mile walk within the counties of Lancashire and Yorkshire, the route of which connects three preserved steam railways – the East Lancashire, the Keighley and Worth Valley and the Embsay to Bolton Abbey.

The walk begins at Ramsbottom's ELR station and finishes at Embsay, and is divided into 16 linked circular stages ranging between 4 and 9.5 miles.

With the inclusion of return routes, the walk enables almost any active family or individual walker the choice to plan their own schedule by combining successive stages in a single day's walk, or by using the railways and/or local or individual transport, to walk the route in its entirety over a period of time.

The walk can also commence at Embsay station by first walking the return routes and then the Heritage Trail to regain the starting points.

In its journey, the trail offers as much variety as possible, taking in the wonderful countryside of Lancashire and Yorkshire, contrasting with the history and remnants of the industrial revolution. There are moorland sections, cloughs, valleys, riverside paths, green lanes, packhorse routes, bridleways and old quarry tracks, all of which are public rights of way, or where access is free to all. Although the highest altitude gained is only 429 metres (on Top of Stairs) outstanding views from every hilltop over the surrounding countryside will be discovered.

The flat moorland sections contain areas of course grass, bog and cotton grass and are the haunt of curlew, lapwing and grouse. On the lower slopes, a more acidic grass, along with heather, gorse and bilberry can be seen, whilst in the river sections, glimpses of heron, mallard, dipper, wagtail and the occasional kingfisher can be spotted if you are lucky.

The history of the three preserved railways has been well documented in detailed books and journals available at retail outlets, and so a brief account of the dedication and hard work by the various groups of volunteers who brought about their rebirth is history in itself, and is recorded at various stages throughout the guide.

Tom Schofield
March 2010

The Heritage Trail in Brief

Stage 1	East Lancs Railway station, Ramsbottom - Bury Old Road - Windy Harbour - Balladen - Townsend Fold - Rawtenstall station
Return	Townsend Fold - Irwell Vale - Strongstry - Stubbins Vale - Springwood - Ramsbottom
Stage 2	Rawtenstall station - Waingate - Chapel Hill - Myrtle Earth - Seat Naze - Newchurch - Waterfoot.
Return	Waterfoot - Myrtle Grove - Cloughfold - Hall Carr - Rawtenstall
Stage 3	Waterfoot - The Hile - Maden Lodge - Bacup
Return	Maden Lodge - Stacksteads - Rake Head - Waterfoot
Stage 4	Bacup - Todmorden Old Road - Sharneyford
Return	Sharneyford - Heald Top - Deerplay - Lane Head - Higher Broad Clough - Bacup
Stage 5	Sharneyford - Limersgate - Gorpley Clough - Stones Wood - Gauxholme - Todmorden
Return	Todmorden Edge End - Sourhall - Flowerscar - Sharneyford
Stage 6	Todmorden - Ewood - Cat Hole - Whirlaw Stones - Great Rock - Hippins - Blackshaw Head - Jack Bridge
Return	Jack Bridge - Jumble Hole Clough - Rodwell End - Rochdale Canal, Todmorden

Stage 7 Jack Bridge – Strines – Standing Stone Hill – Graining Water – Blake Dean Bridge – Hardcastle Craggs – New Bridge

Return New Bridge – Lee Bank – Slack – Colden Water – Jack Bridge

Stage 8 New Bridge – Slurring Rock – Shackleton – Able Cross – Paddock Beck – Grain Water Bridge

Return Grain Water Bridge – Grain Farm – Lumb Bridge – Lower Grimsworth Farm – Smeekin Hill – New Bridge

Stage 9 Grain Water Bridge – Top of Stairs – Lower Fold Farm – Moor Side Lane – Marsh – Oxenhope station (KWVR)

Return Oxenhope station – Top of Stones – Rag Beck – Hebden Road (A6033) – Roms Clough – White Hole Farm – Grain Water Bridge

Stage 10 Oxenhope station – Old Oxenhope Hall – Hole Farm – Howarth Parsonage – Howarth station – Mytholmes Lane – Oakworth station

Return Oakworth station – Vale Mill Lane – Hebden Road – Brow Top – Blackmoor Lane – Delf Hill – Lower Hayley – Dark Lane – Oxenhope station

Stage 11 Oakworth station – Providence Mill – Tim Lane – Newsholme – Cat Clough – Newsholme Dean – Goose Eye

Return Goose Eye – Holme House – Higher Lathe – Slack Lane – Holden Park – Larkfield House – Oakworth station

Stage 12 Goose Eye – Clough Bank – Pole Stoop – America Farm – Lumb Clough – Sutton

Return Sutton – Eastburn Crag – Whitley Head – Lower Redcar – Tarn Lane – Laycock – Goose Eye

Stage 13	Sutton - Glusburn - Kildwick - Jubilee Tower - Great Slack - Tar Topping - Low Bracken Hill Farm - Silsden
Return	Silsden - Leeds/Liverpool Canal - Silsden Bridge - Lyon Farm - Holme Beck - Sutton
Stage 14	Silsden - Leeds/Liverpool Canal - Brunthwaite - Swartha - North End - Nab End - Moorside Lane - Gildersber Farm - Addingham
Return	Addingham - Marchup Beck - Parsons Lane - Walton Hole - Foster Cliff House - Ivy House - Hey Hills - Silsden
Stage 15	Addingham - Low Laithe - Beech House - Howber Hill - Bowers Barn - Beamsley - Bolton Bridge - Bolton Abbey station (Embsay/Bolton Abbey Railway)
Return	Bolton Abbey station - Haw Pike Farm - Highfield - Addingham Golf Course - Sugar Hill - Addingham
Stage 16	Bolton Abbey station - Halton East - Calm Slate Farm - Eastby - Embsay station
Return	Embsay station - Water Lane Laithe - Draughton - Haynholme Farm - Bolton Abbey station

The East Lancashire Railway Preservation Society

The ELR Preservation Society was first formed in 1968, originally to reopen a section of line from Stubbins Junction to Accrington, their headquarters being the abandoned station at Helmshore. However, after four years hard work, they had to abandon this idea and turned their attention to the valley line between Bury and Rawtenstall.

Initially, they opened the Bury Transport Museum at Castlecroft, as British Rail were still running an occasional coal train to Rawtenstall. Meanwhile, the Society concentrated its efforts on fund raising and running brake van rides in the yard at Castlecroft.

At the end of the 1970s, British Rail announced that the freight service was to end, and the track was to be removed. The Society had to act fast to negotiate the purchase of the line and after a great deal of hard work and invaluable help from local councils, finance was raised and the line acquired in 1985. The gigantic task had now begun with the reinstatement of the four miles of track between Bury and Ramsbottom, and after over twenty years of unstoppable ambition, the volunteers' dream came to fruition, when on the 25th July 1987, a train consisting of six maroon carriages filled with dignitaries and guests, and hauled by No. 32 Gothenburg and ex-Burnley gas works No. 1, left Bolton Street station bound for Summerseat and Ramsbottom.

Since that day, the railway has succeeded in extending to Irwell Vale and Rawtenstall in 1992, and to Heywood in 2002, giving the line a total length of 12 miles, and providing a link to the main line, initiating occasional interesting excursions to various destinations.

Ramsbottom

The butt of many a comedian's joke, Ramsbottom actually translates into 'valley of the wild garlic'. Its development from scattered farmsteads into a small industrial town is attributed to three families – the Peels, the Grants and the Ashtons. Sir Robert Peel Snr. and William Yates built the Old Ground works in 1783, which was situated roughly inside the area now bounded by Central Street, Bridge Street, Square Street and Smithy Brow.

The son of Robert Peel, also Sir Robert, became the more famous on becoming the Prime Minister in 1841, and was noted for the repeal of the corn laws and the founding of the London Police Force. Peel Monument on Holcombe moor was erected in his memory in 1851.

Also in the year 1783, the Grant family of Strathspey in Scotland, moved south to Lancashire where William and his three sons, William, John and Daniel began work at a calico printing works in Bury, until the three sons set up in business themselves in Manchester. In 1806, they purchased the Old Ground works in Ramsbottom from the firm of Peel and Yates. The brothers then went on to build the 'Square' calico print works in 1821 (this being aptly named as its external dimensions were 241 x 241 feet). Charles, the youngest brother, born in Lancashire, died in 1805. Daniel and William became known as the Cheeryble brothers, believed to have been the inspiration for the brothers in Charles Dickens' 'Nicholas Nickleby'.

Ramsbottom Station

Today, the town having lost most of its industrial past, still retains much of its heritage, and a new breath of life has returned since the re-opening of the East Lancashire Railway in 1987. Open-air markets were reintroduced, businesses old and new flourished, with tourism replacing manufacturing.

Every weekend in December, Dickensian street markets are held, creating a taste of yesteryear with stallholders and shopkeepers dressed in Victorian costume, and brass bands heralding the spirit of the festive season.

More information about the town and its history can be obtained from the Heritage Centre, situated in Carr Street opposite the library.

Stage 1: Ramsbottom to Rawtenstall

Start	Ramsbottom ELR Station GR 793167
Distance	4 miles (6.5 km) linear 8.5 miles (13.5 km) circular
Maps	OS Explorer 287 OL21
Parking	ELR station

Turn right out of the station entrance and right again over the level crossing. Cross the road, noting the picnic area between the ELR and the River Irwell. Cross over the river and then immediately turn left into Kenyon Street, which leads through an industrial area, after which, turn right into a briefly enclosed footway. Then a metal kissing gate sends the path across pastureland to come alongside the River Irwell. Head upstream, shortly crossing a footbridge, over a side beck, and then a kissing gate which gives access to a large field. Continue ahead keeping to the right hand boundary, which is at first a hedge to soon become vertical flagstones with causey stones underfoot. Pass through a kissing gate and then turn immediately right. Now rise up the track with a large farm building on your right. At the first junction, continue ahead but now on a surfaced lane that ascends to cross airily over the M66 motorway (note the drill marks in the rock face - evidence of the blasting required in the construction of the cutting). At the T-junction, turn left to advance up the lane, which soon gains the A56 road. Cross and turn left to pass the Duckworth Arms, known locally as the 'Bunk'. In 100 metres, turn right into Hollins Lane (track) which is firstly enclosed by holly bushes, then angles left where vestiges of stone cobbles are visible.

At the next junction, turn left into Bury Old Road, which is followed for 300 metres to meet the A680. Cross and turn left and after 150 metres go right into Michael Wife's Lane, which is in fact a continuation of Bury Old Road. After passing a charming bungalow on the right, the route delves into a leafy enclosed way that descends to a ford and footbridge crossing Plunge Beck, a delectable spot. Cross to continue ahead, rising up the sunken stony track under a canopy of leaves. Eventually the trail levels and becomes surfaced. The driveway going off to the right leads

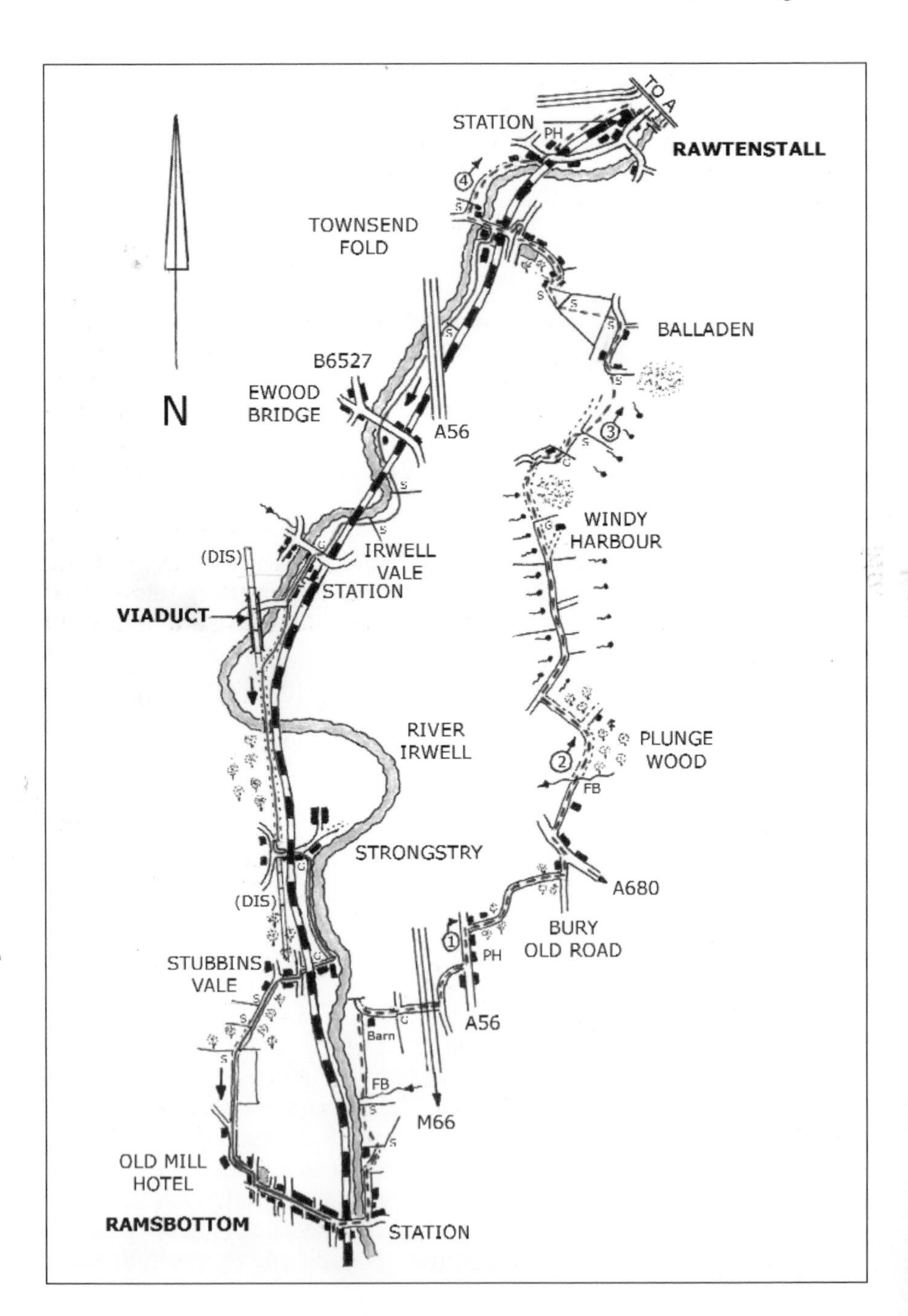
TO A
STATION
PH
RAWTENSTALL
4
TOWNSEND
FOLD
BALLADEN
B6527
EWOOD
BRIDGE
A56
3
N
WINDY
HARBOUR
(DIS)
IRWELL
VALE
STATION
VIADUCT
RIVER
IRWELL
PLUNGE
WOOD
2
FB
STRONGSTRY
A680
(DIS)
BURY
OLD ROAD
1
PH
STUBBINS
VALE
A56
Barn
FB
M66
OLD MILL
HOTEL
RAMSBOTTOM
STATION

up to the site of New Hall, dated 1538, the home of the Rawsthorne family. Little now remains of the building, the site presently is owned by the Waterworks Utility Company. At the next junction, turn right. (The left turn - Gincroft Lane, leads down into the village of Edenfield). Rise up the sunken Bury Old Road, which turns left as the gradient eases. There now follows a fine panoramic walk with views over the lower Rossendale Valley, with Peel Monument and the west Pennine moors beyond.

Ahead now, the prominent property known as Windy Harbour (or Lower Carcroft) comes into view. Ignore its access drive and continue ahead to pass through two gates. The old road now passes through the remains of Horncliffe quarry. The large house, seen amongst the trees below, is Horncliffe House, built for the Hardman family around 1870 and now converted into a hotel and restaurant named, Horncliffe Mansion.

Go through a cleft to arrive at a junction. Keep ahead and enter the yard at Horncliffe Top Farm, dated 1681. The building was originally the old Quarryman's Inn, situated on Bury Old Road before the turnpike road was constructed below. Pass the front of the building and round to the

Windy Harbour

left onto a rough track. After 30 metres pass over a stile on the right. We are now back on the line of the old Bury Road, which is soon discernable as a sunken hollow way that descends to come alongside a disused quarry, with a stile on its edge. Now enter a walled lane which turns right and becomes surfaced.

In 300 metres, enter the hamlet of Balladen where a short detour to the right will reveal Balladen Old Hall, dated 1687. Returning to the lane, take the path on the left, pass through a kissing gate to follow a faint path across pastureland. Cross a slight depression to find vestiges of causey stones. The path now rises to come alongside a crumbling wall. Pass through a second kissing gate and descend a rough field towards housing below. Pass through a gate and then alongside the boundary of a garden to find a flight of steps. Descend and turn right onto a cinder track with a block of garages to the right. Pass through a tight gap between a gate stump and lamp-post to enter Lower Clowes. The lane now becomes surfaced and is followed down to the A682. Turn right and, in 60 metres, cross and turn left down Holme Lane, which advances to meet the ELR at Townsend Fold level crossing. (Those wishing to follow the return route to Ramsbottom, a description of which follows later, should turn left after the crossing. If returning by train, continue on the Heritage Trail). Continue ahead, soon passing over the River Irwell via Holme Bridge, to gain the hamlet of Holme. After the first cottage, turn right to find a kissing gate to the left of a second cottage. Now follow the riverside path until reaching the Groundwork Countryside Centre, where there are picnic areas, a shop and café. Leave the Centre by passing beneath the archway of Hardman's Mill with its galleried chimney. On emerging from the archway, cross New Hall Hey Road with the Cobblers Inn on the left. On reaching the level crossing, take the path to the left of the signal box, which we follow, with the ELR on the right, along to Rawtenstall station.

Return Route

Townsend Fold to Ramsbottom

From the level crossing at Townsend Fold, turn left with the ELR on your left. At the entrance to K Steels, pass through the gap to the right of the main gates. Follow the signs round the perimeter of the factory site to come alongside the River Irwell. The riverside path is now followed passing beneath the Edenfield by-pass to arrive at Ewood Bridge and the B6527. Ewood Bridge was rebuilt in 1846 on top of the original structure, which dates from 1790. Rise up the slope and steps and then cross the

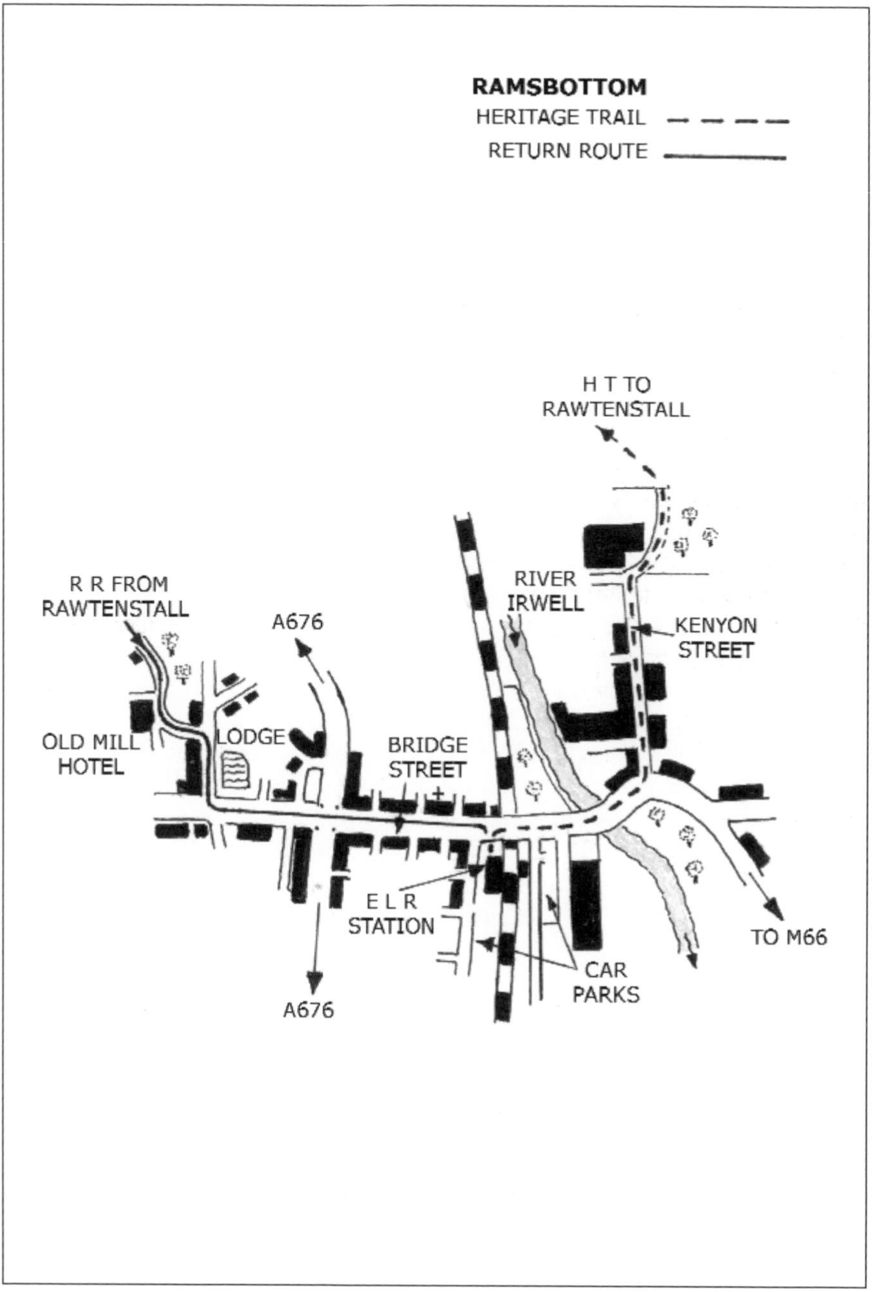

RAMSBOTTOM
HERITAGE TRAIL
RETURN ROUTE
H T TO RAWTENSTALL
R R FROM RAWTENSTALL
A676
RIVER IRWELL
KENYON STREET
OLD MILL HOTEL
LODGE
BRIDGE STREET
E L R STATION
CAR PARKS
TO M66
A676

road to descend the hand-railed steps back onto the riverside. Follow the path round the boundary of the football clubhouse and pitches – now in a state of disrepair. Pass beneath the railway bridge. Cross two stiles and then ascend a flight of steps up to a kissing gate. Now the way drops down again to gain the riverside. Negotiate two kissing gates on either side of a further railway bridge to enter a tightly enclosed path, with the ELR on the left. At its end, pass through the gate and turn right to enter Irwell Vale. (The station is now up to the left for those wishing to return by train).

Continue ahead into Meadow Way with the river on the right. When the road turns right to pass over Lumb Bridge, continue ahead onto the riverside path and cycleway. Across the river is Lumb viaduct, which carried the Stubbins Junction/Accrington line – closed in 1966. Ignoring the path going left through the subway, rise up the surfaced path onto the leafy, disused trackbed that is now followed for half a mile with the ELR running parallel down to the left. When a metal fence is seen ahead, leave the trackbed on the right to descend the lane, then turn left, passing beneath the old line and into the hamlet of Strongstry.

Continue ahead under a second bridge, carrying the ELR, and immediately after, go right to pass through a kissing gate onto the enclosed riverside path.

Irwell Vale

The playing field, on the opposite bank, was the site of the Chatterton Riots in 1826, when men and women hand weavers believed that the arrival of power looms would make them redundant. Thomas Aitken's mill which stood on the site was attacked and looms were destroyed. The army was then deployed and shots were fired, resulting in the death of one woman and six men as well as numerous woundings. Rioters were either imprisoned or deported to Australia.

At the far end of the riverside path, pass through the kissing gate, turn right to pass in front of housing, then under the subway beneath the ELR, noting the disused entrance steps on the left. On emerging, turn left, then first right into Stubbins Street, the oldest part of the village. The two cottages on the right are 400 years old. At the junction, turn left, rising up the stony track with Springfield House on the right. As the track levels, go over the stile and enter the National Trust's Stubbins Estate. Follow the metal railings down into a small valley. Now ascend up through the trees to a stile in the left hand fence. Advance along the tightly enclosed path through pastureland that soon emerges onto an access drive. Continue ahead passing Top Wood on the right and then emerge into the car park at The Old Mill Hotel. Follow its access drive down to Springwood Street and turn right. On the left is Devil Hole Lodge which once served Carr Mill - long since demolished. At the junction, turn left down Carr Street, passing the Library and Heritage Centre, to arrive at the traffic lights. The Tilted Urn on the left is a part of the Irwell Valley's Sculpture Trail. Continue ahead into Bridge Street, at the bottom of which is Ramsbottom station.

Rawtenstall/Rossendale

Rawtenstall, along with Haslingden, Bacup and Whitworth make up the Borough of Rossendale, known locally as the Valley. Actually the borough boasts two valleys – the Irwell and the Spodden. The valley sides rise steeply from the ground to a gently sloping green terrace, beyond which the land again rises to the summit of the moors. These terraces were prime areas for the deforestation which began around 1500, the inhabitants being paid 4d. for every acre cleared. It was from these farms and smallholdings that the initial woollen industry began. Families would spin the wool from their own sheep, often in the upstairs rooms of their cottages. The yarn was woven into cloth on handlooms, a process which continued until the arrival of mechanisation, brought about by the inventions of John Kay (flying shuttle), James Hargreaves (spinning jenny) and Richard Arkwright (water frame).

Thus the Industrial Revolution was born.

With its high rainfall, Rossendale was an ideal area to harness the power of water. By 1830 there were fifty spinning mills in Rossendale, all driven by water.

Weavers Cottage

By 1844 this had risen to eighty, along with ten calico printing mills. The cotton industry continued to expand until its recession in the 1930s and, since then, a gradual decline, not helped by cheap overseas labour, has taken place.

Today, Rawtenstall is in the process of re-invention with the restoration of the East Lancashire Railway, a first class ski slope at Ski Rossendale, new facilities planned for Marl Pitts Leisure Centre, rebuilding of the town centre, and is host to the countries biggest motor-cycle show. The town is moving on to a new revolution – the tourist industry!

Stage 2: Rawtenstall to Waterfoot

Start	Rawtenstall ELR station GR 809225
Distance	2.25 miles (3.5 km) linear 4 miles (6.5 km) circular
Map	OS Explorer OL21
Parking	Rawtenstall station

From the station entrance, turn left and then cross the road via the sanctuary island. Continue ahead over the footbridge and then turn left. Follow the footpath round the car park into Bocholt Way. At the end of the footpath go over the road, again using the sanctuary island. Pass over the River Irwell by the old bridg,e which was the route of the Bury to Rawtenstall old road, dating from the 18th century. Turn right into Bacup Road, passing the bus station on the right (soon to be relocated), and the cricket ground on the left. Opposite is Weaver's Cottage, a museum, with its 'taking in' steps to the upper floor where the cloth was woven. The south elevation is the more appealing, with its mullioned windows to allow maximum light for the weavers, the living area being on the ground floor.

Turn left immediately after the cricket field to pass through two impressive gateposts, dated 1864, and up the driveway which originally lead to Greenbank House. On reaching new housing, turn left up the enclosed path. At the top, turn left into Grange Road and then first right into Alder Street. Now turn left into Springfield Road and, in 20 metres, find a briefly enclosed entry on the right. This emerges into Nuttall Street. Now go directly over Newchurch Road into Waingate Road (track). Follow the road with a stream on the right. The track soon narrows into a leafy way and rises to arrive at the charming hamlet of Waingate. Turn left at the end of a short beech hedge onto a stone flagged path, soon meeting a quiet lane. Turn right. Now ascend, keeping right at the Y-junction. Pass Chapel Hill Farm on the right and then the 'Friends' burial ground, dated 1665, the walls being rebuilt in 1817.

Continue ahead at the next junction soon passing the impressively restored Meadow Head. As the track turns left, take the stile or gate on the right. Pause here to admire the view back down to the Rossendale

Burial Ground

Valley with Cowpe Lowe beyond. Follow the well defined path downhill, which soon enters newly planted woodland, where glimpses of sports fields, part of Marl Pitts leisure complex, will be seen on the right. On reaching a junction, take the stile on the left and ascend the enclosed track up to the livery stables. Go over the stile seen ahead, then walk up the pasture to a further stile, which gives access onto the driveway to Myrtle Earth Farm. Turn right away from the farm, ignore the lane going off to the right and rise towards the trees seen ahead. The track turns left to come alongside the woodland and a stone wall. At the corner of the trees and wall, go over the stile on the right into a large meadow. Now follow the wall, eventually arriving at a further stile. Cross and go down to a stone post on the edge of Seat Naze. There are more good views from here up the Rossendale Valley toward Bacup, and up the side valley to Lumb and Water, with Deerplay Moor beyond.

Turn right and start to descend, now on a distinct path, ignoring any paths to right or left. Soon you will enter a sunken, leafy section and then the path becomes enclosed and enters Newchurch village. Cross the road and take the lane descending to the left of The Boars Head. On the left is

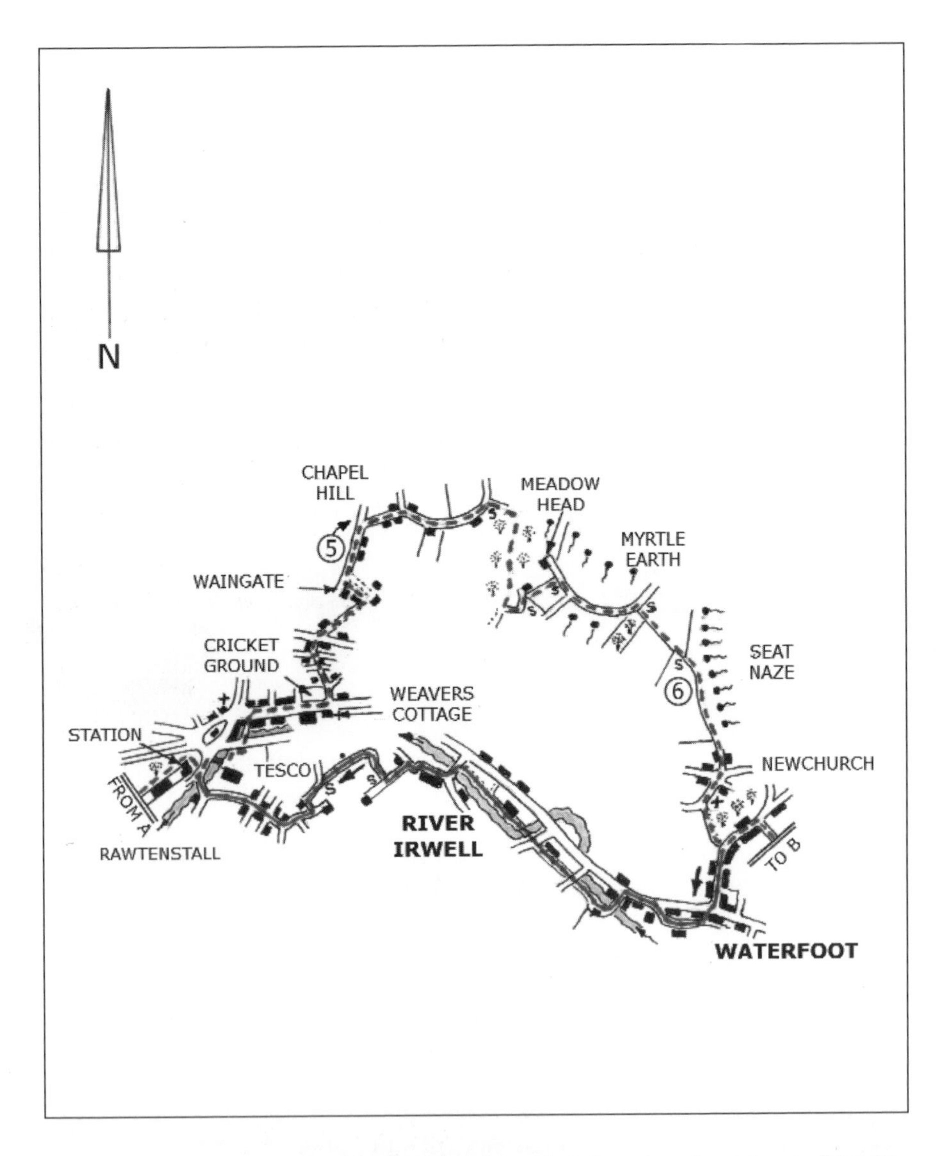

St. Nicholas and St. John's Church (there has been a church on this site since 1511). As the lane turns right look for a cobbled path on the left. Follow this down through woodland to emerge into Burnley Road East at Waterfoot. The Heritage Trail turns left here. For the return to Rawtenstall, turn right.

Return Route

Waterfoot to Rawtenstall

Go down Burnley Road East to the traffic lights at Waterfoot. Cross and turn right. In 50 metres go left up a narrow entrance with the Duke of Buccleugh on your right. Emerge into Stansfield Road and turn right. The original East Lancs Railway line passed through here on the route to Bacup until its closure in 1966. At the end of Stansfield Road, turn left into Bacup Road. After 300 metres turn left into Holt Mill Road and then through the mill underpass to cross over the bridge spanning the River Irwell.

Follow the path round to the right to come alongside the river, which brings us onto the old ELR trackbed once more. Follow the obvious path, crossing over two access lanes, after which the route has been recently renovated – one section for walkers and cyclists, the other for horses. At the end of this section (Cloughfold) turn left over the river, and then immediately right. Follow the road round a double bend and in 100 metres, arrive at Union Terrace. Turn left up the arrow-straight access

Isolated Chimney

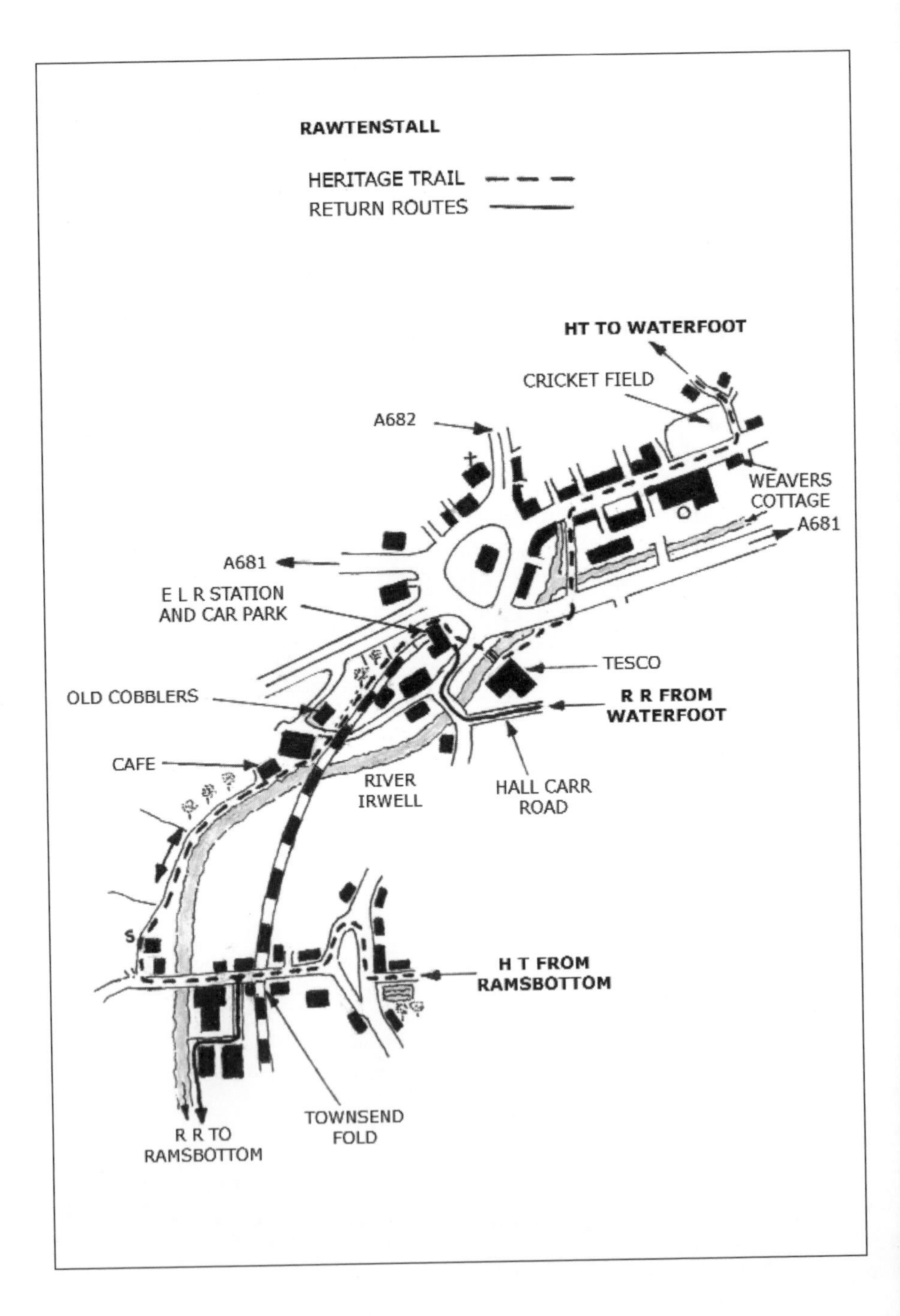
RAWTENSTALL
HERITAGE TRAIL
RETURN ROUTES
HT TO WATERFOOT
CRICKET FIELD
A682
WEAVERS COTTAGE
A681
A681
E L R STATION AND CAR PARK
TESCO
OLD COBBLERS
R R FROM WATERFOOT
CAFE
RIVER IRWELL
HALL CARR ROAD
S
H T FROM RAMSBOTTOM
R R TO RAMSBOTTOM
TOWNSEND FOLD

drive and, on nearing the house, turn right into the signed Bridleway. Soon a solitary chimney will be met, which was built in this position to gain height, thus saving the expense of building a much taller structure in the valley below.

At the end of the bridleway go over the stile on the left, then up the driveway. Turn left just before the house and ascend a narrow path, squeezing between holly bushes and a fence, to arrive at Middle Hall Carr. Turn right down the access track to pass Hall Carr Farm on the right and then continue ahead down Hall Carr Road. Turn right at the bottom, cross over the River Irwell to find Rawtenstall station situated to your left.

Newchurch/Waterfoot

Newchurch, one of the earliest settlements in Rossendale, is situated on the gently sloping terrace above the village of Waterfoot.. Originally built as a chapel of ease to Whalley Abbey, St. Nichols was built in 1511, rebuilt in 1560, and enlarged in 1753, though most of the present building dates from 1825.

A path used on stage two of the Heritage Trail leads from just below the church down to the village of Waterfoot, which sits at the meeting of Whitewell Brook and the River Irwell. The village boasts an elegant glazed arcade, financed by Mr. H. Tricket, a former Alderman and Mayor of Rossendale, who was knighted for his services to the borough.

The East Lancashire Railway extended its line from Rawtenstall to Waterfoot in 1848, where a station was built, originally named Newchurch. It was a further four years before the route was extended to Bacup. A little beyond Waterfoot, the Irwell valley narrowed considerably at a point known as The Glen, and was already occupied by the road and river. The solution to this problem was to construct two tunnels into the hillside for the single track line, named Newchurch No.1 and No.2. With a rapid increase in traffic, it was decided to double the line, but widening the existing tunnels was rejected in favour of a parallel tunnel, measuring 592 yards and named Newchurch No.3, which was completed in 1881.

On stage three of the Heritage Trail's return route, it is still possible to walk through the (290 yard) No.2 tunnel, the remaining two now being sealed off.

Stage 3: Waterfoot to Bacup

Start	**Burnley Road East (B6328) Waterfoot GR 834221**
Distance	**2 miles (3.2 km) linear 4 miles (6.5 km) circular**
Map	**OS Explorer OL21**
Parking	**Waterfoot centre**

Turn left up Burnley Road East and, in 200 metres, go right into Booth Road. Turn left into Todd Carr Road and at its end, go right up the hand railed cobbled path. On emerging out onto the road, turn left and in 50 metres, go left into Siss Clough Park. Follow the driveway round to the right, then turn uphill, passing the tennis courts on your left. At the top, exit the park onto Edgeside Road and go up the lane directly opposite. On reaching the entrance to Farm Hill Farm, go through the gate to the right of the driveway gates. Continue up the enclosed path passing the house/farm, then continue in the same direction on a gravel track. When this angles left, go over the stile seen ahead into pastureland. The path is quite obvious, following the same boundary but changing sides on two occasions.

The high point up to the left is the Hile at 335 metres, with wonderful views of the Rossendale Valley on the right. Cross the access track up to West Hile Farm, with the boundary on your right, and then through a gateway. Now watch carefully for a stile on the right about 30 metres before the field corner. Cross, turn left, then go over a substantial stone step-stile. Continue in the same direction, soon crossing over the track up to East Hile Farm. Soon the path becomes enclosed, passing through three gates. Finally, pass over a stile into rough pasture. Follow the obvious path, crossing a stile and a flagstone footbridge. Rise up the bank to find a junction of tracks. Take the enclosed track ahead which soon passes Top o'th Bank Farm, followed by Bacup Golf Course on the left and playing fields to the right. On reaching the entrance to Maden Lodge Recreation Centre, the Heritage Trail continues ahead down the tree-lined avenue. (**Note** – at this point the return route to Waterfoot turns off to the right.) Continue down the avenue, passing the golf

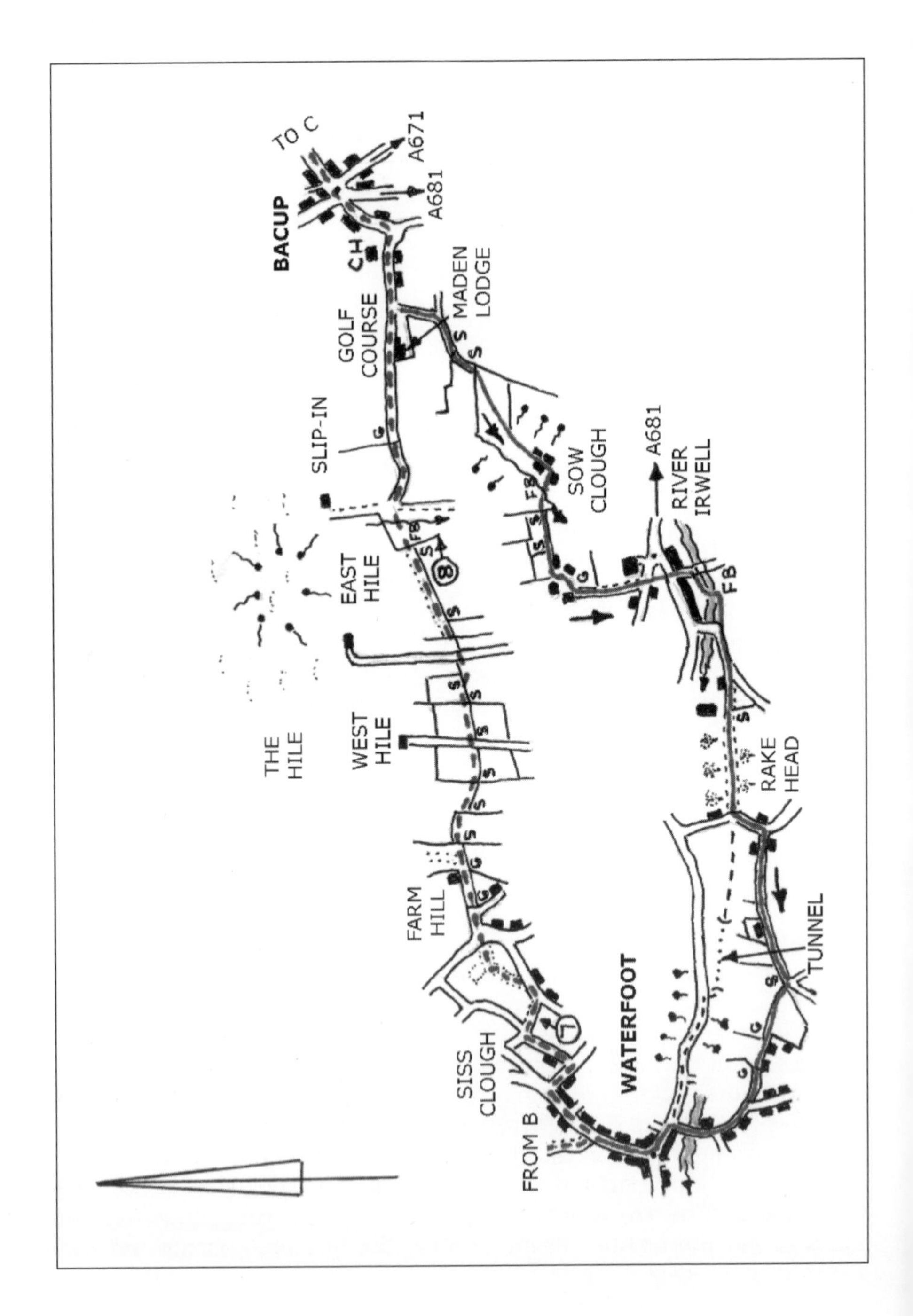
TO C
A671
A681
BACUP
CH
GOLF COURSE
MADEN LODGE
SLIP-IN
SOW CLOUGH
A681
RIVER IRWELL
FB
THE HILE
EAST HILE
WEST HILE
RAKE HEAD
FARM HILL
TUNNEL
WATERFOOT
SISS CLOUGH
FROM B

Maden Lodge

clubhouse on the left. When the road bends to the right, go down the steps on your left and then turn left, descending Bankside Lane to the roundabout at Bacup town centre.

The Return Route

Bacup to Waterfoot

Pass the entrance gates to Maden Lodge into the enclosed path which is followed, turning right round the playing field, then left with pastureland to each side. At the end, go over the stile. Now angle half right away from the boundary, descending to the opposite corner. Continue down the valley, now on a stony track that soon arrives at the stables at Sow Clough Farm. Go through the gate and turn immediately right between the barn and farmhouse. Descend to the footbridge, after which angle left to find stone steps and a stile. Cross and follow the leafy path beneath the tree line. Pass over a stile, turn left round the barn and then turn right into the yard at Honey Hole Farm. Turn left up towards a gate to find a stile on the right. Pass through, turning left into

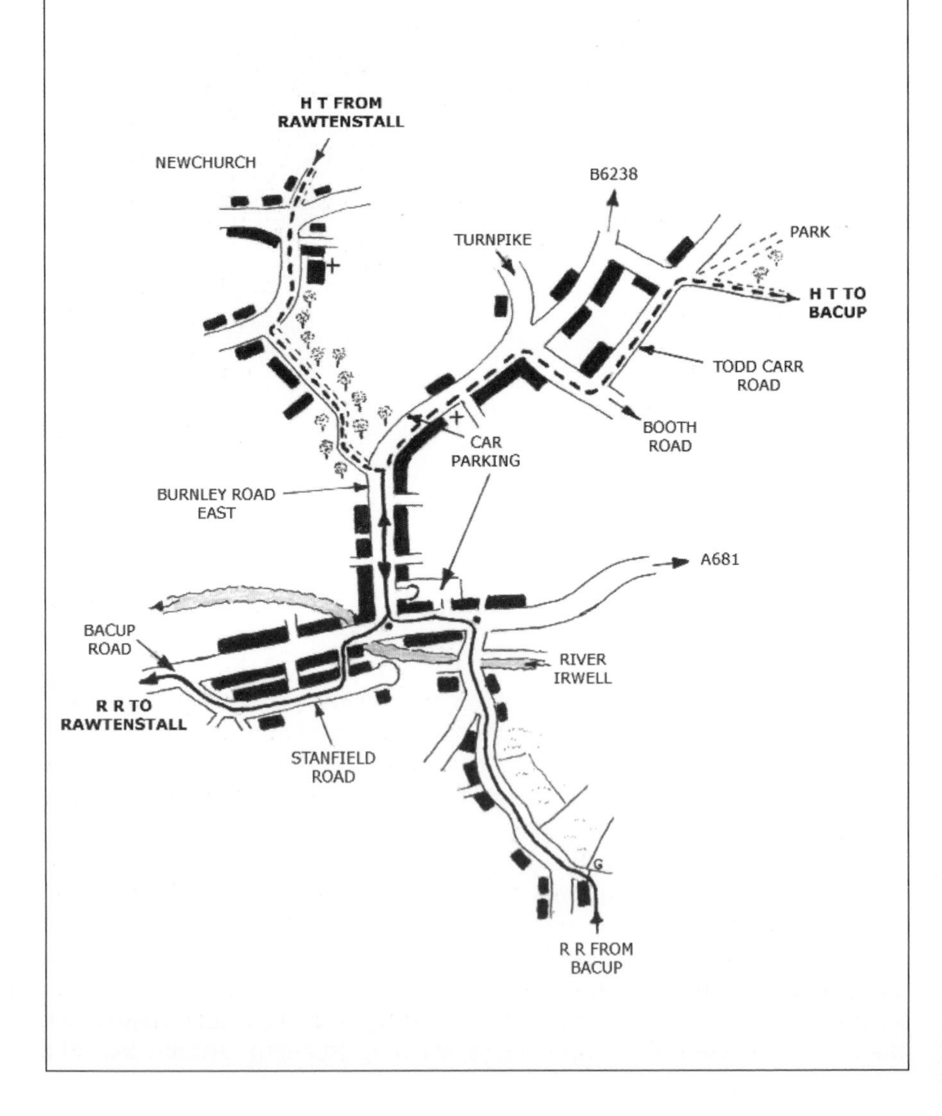
WATERFOOT
HERITAGE TRAIL
RETURN ROUTES
H T FROM RAWTENSTALL
NEWCHURCH
B6238
TURNPIKE
PARK
H T TO BACUP
TODD CARR ROAD
BOOTH ROAD
CAR PARKING
BURNLEY ROAD EAST
A681
BACUP ROAD
RIVER IRWELL
R R TO RAWTENSTALL
STANFIELD ROAD
G
R R FROM BACUP

Newchurch Tunnel

a walled bridleway. After 250 metres, the way becomes surfaced with housing on the right and a school to the left.

On reaching Newchurch Road, cross and continue down the cobbled path, which is to the left of house No. 20. At the next road (Bacup Road) cross and go down the lane to the left of the Rose and Bowl Restaurant. On reaching the River Irwell, turn right through the kissing gate. Follow the riverside path, passing over the footbridge, then turn right to emerge onto Blackwood Road. Go uphill for 150 metres to take the path off to the right, signed Irwell Valley Way. After passing over a stile, the path soon turns right and descends to join the old trackbed of the ELR line from Waterfoot to Bacup. Follow the obvious path to Rake Head Lane (signed Glen Top Playing Field). You now have a choice of routes: If you carry a torch, and are not concerned about the darkness, you can continue ahead to pass through Newchurch No. 2 tunnel and then down Bacup Road back to Waterfoot. The second option is to turn left up Rake

Head Lane, rise steeply and then take the first turning on the right (Royds Road), an unsurfaced byway.

When the track comes alongside a football field on the right, continue through the gate seen ahead. Now turn immediately right, still with the sports ground over the wall on your right. Go over a stile and then keep to the left hand boundary to the rear of housing. Pass through a gate and then down the track to emerge into Carr Lane. Turn right and follow the lane down to its junction with the A681. Turn left and, in a few metres, arrive back at Waterfoot centre. Turn right at the traffic lights into Burnley Road East.

Bacup

The first reference to coal mining in the Rossendale area was made in 1612, mainly based in the hills above Bacup. By 1820, seven coal mines were in operation, some of which were the drift mine type. Lead has also been mined in the area, evidence having been found on Thievely Pike, which lies to the north of Bacup. The major extraction of natural resources from these uplands, over the years, has been the quarrying of stone – the famous Haslingden flagstone, found in quarries throughout Rossendale, has been used in almost every town and city in the country. Indeed, Trafalgar Square in London has in recent years been re-paved using these flagstones for a second time. Another industry associated with Bacup and Rawtenstall is the slipper trade, said to have been initiated by Mr. J.W. Rothwell of Waterfoot in 1875. The trade is still thriving today.

For over one hundred years, the Britannia Coconutters have performed their annual boundary to boundary dance. Held on Easter Saturday, the 'Nutters' have

Grinding Wheel

dressed up and danced through Bacup and Stacksteads, in memory of the old miners who would attach coconut shells to their knees, and paint their faces to ward off evil spirits. People from far and wide travel to watch this spectacle where the participants, accompanied by Stacksteads Band, dance for over ten hours to complete the course.

The term 'new line' is still used in the town for the route of the railway between Rochdale and Bacup, which was Bacup's second railway. Opened in 1881 (thirty years after the ELR's line from Bury), it was built over a period of 19 years by the Lancashire and Yorkshire Railway. The line follows the valley of Spodden to its summit at Britannia, 967 feet above sea level, the highest point on the whole LYR system. From here, a rapid descent at 1 in 34 was made to the station at Bacup. The town had its own engine shed and, in 1921, thirty-seven locomotives were housed there. The line to Bury closed for passengers in 1966, but the Rochdale route closed much earlier (for passengers), on the 16th June 1947.

Stage 4: Bacup to Sharneyford

Start	Roundabout – Bacup centre GR 868230
Distance	1.5 miles (2.5 km) linear 5 miles (8 km) circular
Map	OS Explorer OL21
Parking	Bacup centre

Leave the roundabout at Bacup centre taking the Todmorden road (A681). In 40 metres, note the steps on the left, which lead up to Bacup's Wall of History, and the garden containing the Grinding Wheel and Town Stocks. After this diversion, continue up the A681 for 200 metres and then take the hand-railed path ascending on the left that soon merges into

Toll Bar

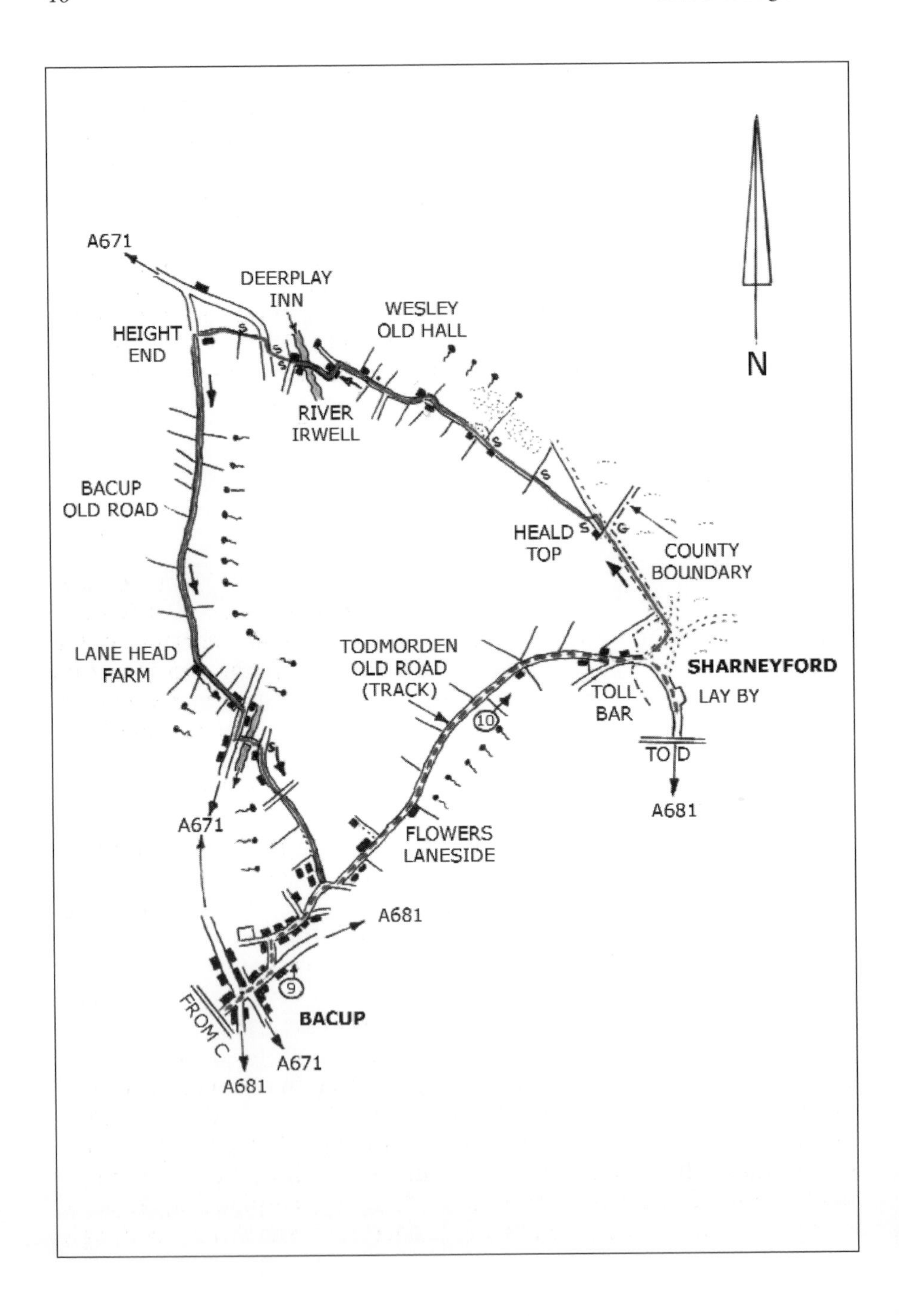
N
A671
DEERPLAY INN
WESLEY OLD HALL
HEIGHT END
RIVER IRWELL
BACUP OLD ROAD
HEALD TOP
COUNTY BOUNDARY
LANE HEAD FARM
TODMORDEN OLD ROAD (TRACK)
SHARNEYFORD
TOLL BAR
LAY BY
10
TO D
A681
A671
FLOWERS LANESIDE
A681
9
FROM C
BACUP
A681
A671

Greensnook Terrace. At the top, turn right passing Windermere Road on the left. In 20 metres, turn left up the narrow lane, Todmorden Old Road (no sign). In 150 metres, note the path going off left with an Irwell Valley Way sign. (You will arrive back here if you take the return route.) Continue up Todmorden Old Road, ignoring a track going off to the right. Pass Laneside Cottages, Flowers Farm and the site of the Old Blue Bell Inn. On approaching Heap Barn, the grade of the old road eases. Pause to admire the view across the valley to Top of Leach, the highest point in Rossendale, with Cowpe Lowe to its right. Soon after passing Heap Hey on the right, the old road descends to the A681. Turn left to cross the county boundary with the toll bar cottage on the left, across from which is the boundary stone at Sharneyford. Here the Heritage Trail and A681 turns right.

The Return Route

Sharneyford to Bacup

The return route continues ahead up Flower Scar Road for 75 metres. and then turns left along the lower track (Rossendale Way), soon arriving at Heald Top Farm (at the time of writing, the conditions underfoot in the environs of the farm were somewhat damp). Pass through two gates into the bridleway. In 20 metres, turn left and wade across the small enclosure to a stile. Turn right to continue between the vestiges of a wall and fence and then over a stile, where conditions now improve. Follow the obvious track with old, overgrown quarry workings (gruffy ground) up to the right. At the next farm, the track turns right, then left to pass through a cutting, where there are good views of Weir village down to the left. Continue following Rossendale Way signs, soon entering an enclosed path, on the right of which is a monument, marking the site of the Heald Wesleyan Chapel and School dated 1832-1868.

Pass Wesley Old Hall and then turn left, dropping down a driveway in front of Old Clough House, to a pleasing corner as the way passes over the infant River Irwell. Rise to where the lane turns left at Clough Hey and then climb the steps and stile directly ahead. Ascend two meadows to gain the A671 road (Bacup/Burnley). Turn right and in 20 metres cross to the footpath sign opposite. With a wall on the right, continue up the field passing to the rear of Height End and out onto the access track, which soon arrives at a junction with Bacup Old Road. (If you require refreshment, turn right to find the Deerplay Inn, only 300 metres along the lane.) If not, turn left. Bacup Old Road runs unfailingly

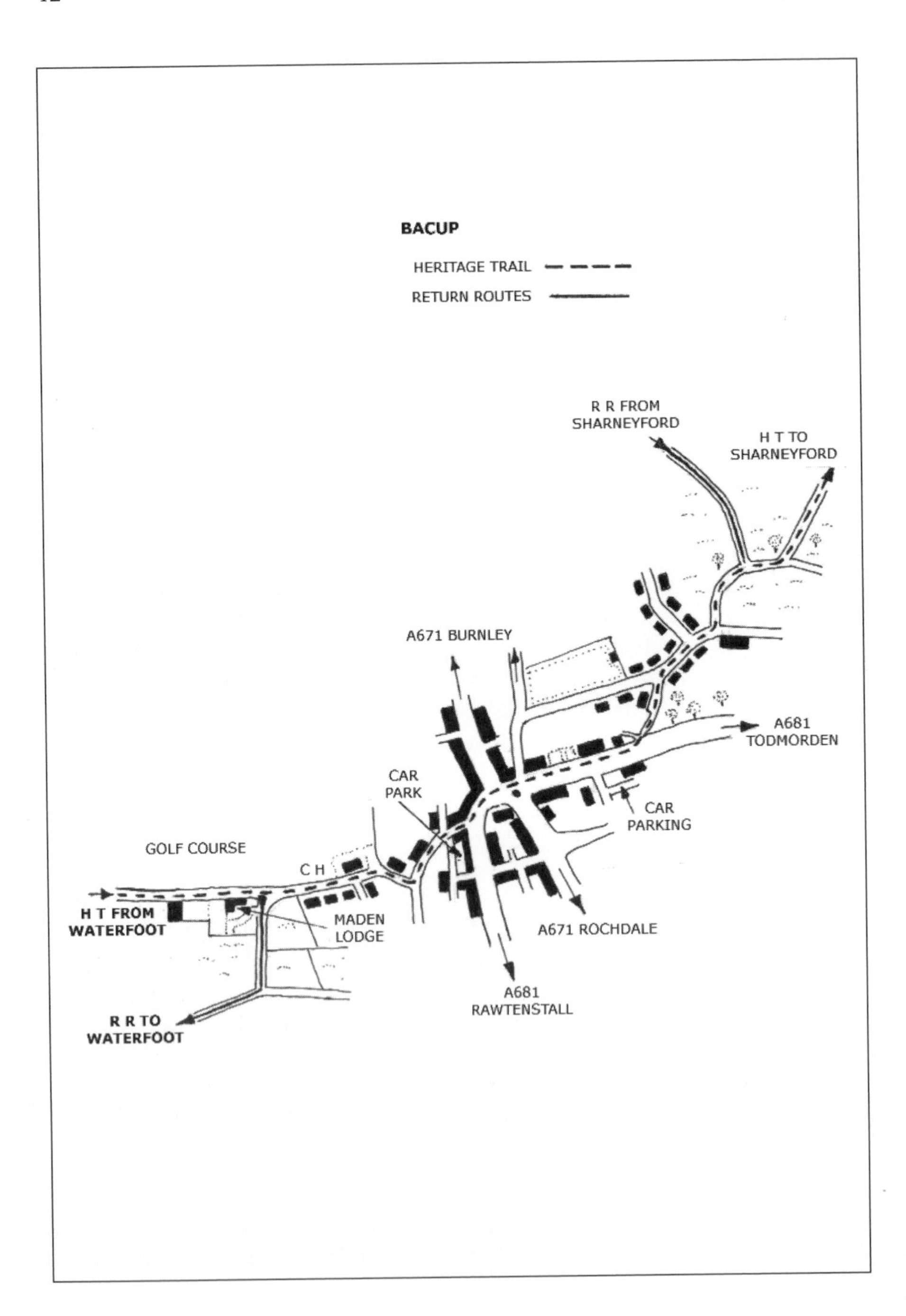
BACUP
HERITAGE TRAIL
RETURN ROUTES
R R FROM SHARNEYFORD
H T TO SHARNEYFORD
A671 BURNLEY
A681 TODMORDEN
CAR PARK
CAR PARKING
GOLF COURSE
C H
H T FROM WATERFOOT
MADEN LODGE
A671 ROCHDALE
A681 RAWTENSTALL
R R TO WATERFOOT

Heald Monument

along the ridge above Weir village and the upper Irwell valley, until reaching Lane Head Farm.

Turning left, the old road descends steeply, with a stream for company on the right, soon emerging onto the A671. Turn right and, in 250 metres, cross the road and then the River Irwell via the footbridge. Rise steeply, with an accompanying wall on the left, to attain the Irwell Valley Way. Turn right following the Way unerringly, passing first beneath an archway carrying a cross-track and then Bacup Borough football ground down to the right. The path now passes behind housing to soon emerge into Todmorden Old Road, mentioned earlier. Turn right and follow the outward route for the quarter mile walk back to Bacup centre.

Stage 5: Sharneyford to Todmorden

Start	**Lay-by (A681) Sharneyford GR 890245**
Distance	**4 miles (6.5 km) linear 7 miles (11.3 km) circular**
Map	**OS Explorer OL21**
Parking	**Lay-by (A681) Sharneyford**

Follow the A681 as it turns right, passing a lay-by on the left. The road now starts to descend. After 400 metres, turn right at a footpath sign and cattle-grid. In 150 metres, the track divides, our route takes the lower one. We are now walking on Limers Gate, an old route trodden by packhorses, taking lime from Clitheroe and wool and cloth from the Burnley/Colne area to markets at Rochdale and Manchester. It's an easy stride along Limers Gate, the original surface probably having been made up of causey stones, now overlaid by more modern materials. Views down to the left open up here, revealing a glimpse of the Astronomy Centre and our next objective, Gorpley Reservoir and Clough, and in the distance, Stoodley Pike on the Pennine Way. Soon a signpost will be met sending Limers Gate slanting off right up the hillside. The Heritage Trail continues ahead for 400 metres to the next signpost indicating a left turn for Gorpley. Follow the wet but well marked path down Counting Hill to eventually turn left and descend into a small gully. Rise up the far side with a wall now on the right. Continue to the ladder-stile seen ahead. Follow the accompanying wall to soon merge onto a Landrover track. Pass through a gate and follow the track. When it turns left, leave it on the right to follow a gully downhill. Down to the right is Gorpley Reservoir. (On the far side of the dam, you may be able to see a path climbing over Inchfield Moor, another packhorse route on its course to Rochdale via the Long Causeway and Wardle.)

The gully terminates at a wall. Go through the small gate and then down the field to a stile leading onto an access track. Continue ahead to the next junction. Turn right to pass round the Water Board buildings to find a sign and gate on the left leading into Gorpley Clough. Descend the steps and follow the delightful path down the clough, alternating from

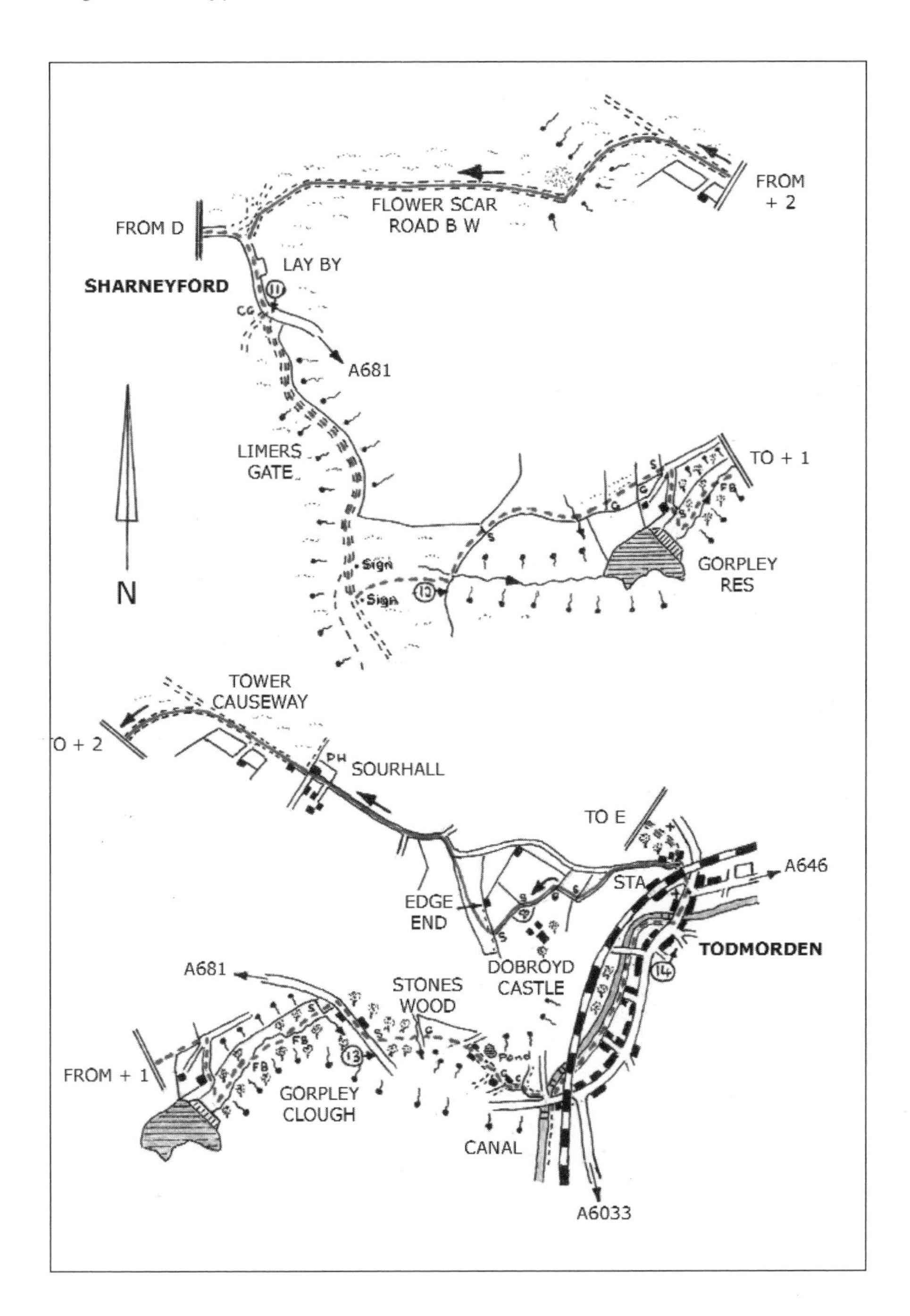
FROM + 2
FLOWER SCAR
ROAD B W
FROM D
LAY BY
SHARNEYFORD
CG
A681
LIMERS
GATE
N
TO + 1
FB
GORPLEY
RES
Sign
Sign
TOWER
CAUSEWAY
TO + 2
PH
SOURHALL
TO E
A646
STA
EDGE
END
TODMORDEN
DOBROYD
CASTLE
A681
STONES
WOOD
FB
FB
Pond
FROM + 1
GORPLEY
CLOUGH
CANAL
A6033

bank to bank via footbridges. Eventually, the path gains the small car park at the A681 road. Turn right to pass Stones House on the left, and after a further 50 metres, cross the road and ascend the steps and over the stile. The path now rises through Stones Wood, crossing over a small side stream to gain a metal kissing gate leading into pastureland.
Follow the obvious path through two gateless gaps to pass to the right of a disused barn and then to the rear of Friths Farm. Now descend the concrete access drive, passing a small pond on the left. When the drive turns sharply right, carry on ahead on a faint path. Pass the isolated chimney, built here to save the expense of a taller structure at the mill below. Continue ahead to the environs of Watt Hole Cottages. Negotiate two small, narrow gates, cross over the drive and then through two more gates to emerge onto a packhorse route named Watty Lane. There are fine views from here up the Walsden valley and across to the Shepherds Rest with Stoodley beyond.

Turn right to descend Watty Lane, noting the old milestone over the wall on the right, which is sadly unreadable. Turn right on gaining Pexwood Road, then left into Bacup Road (A681). Cross immediately, and then pass over the Rochdale Canal. Turn right to gain the towpath turning sharp right to pass under the A681. With luck, the canal should now be on your left. Pass the middle Gauxholme Lock and then under the impressive railway bridge, which is unfortunately in a filthy condition. Continue along the aquatic route to arrive opposite the massive brick retaining wall, built to support the railway above, following a landslip. At the next lock (No. 19), with its electric gate, leave the canal turning left into Rochdale Road and, in 200 metres, arrive at the roundabout in the centre of Todmorden.

The Return Route

Todmorden/Dobroyd/Sourhall – Sharneyford Toll Bar

From the roundabout, follow the Railway Station sign up past the White Hart. Now continue ahead under the railway viaduct. The next stage of the Heritage Trail diverges up Ridge Steps on the right. Our way continues ahead, following Doghouse Lane which zig-zags and rises at an angle of '1 in 4'. Ignoring the footpath sign on the left, continue up the rake for 150 metres and then go left at the stone gatepost into a leafy enclosed way. Advance through the woodland on the obvious path, with improving views of Todmorden on the left. Eventually, a stile sends a faint path out into pastureland, with an accompanying wall to the left. Pass through a

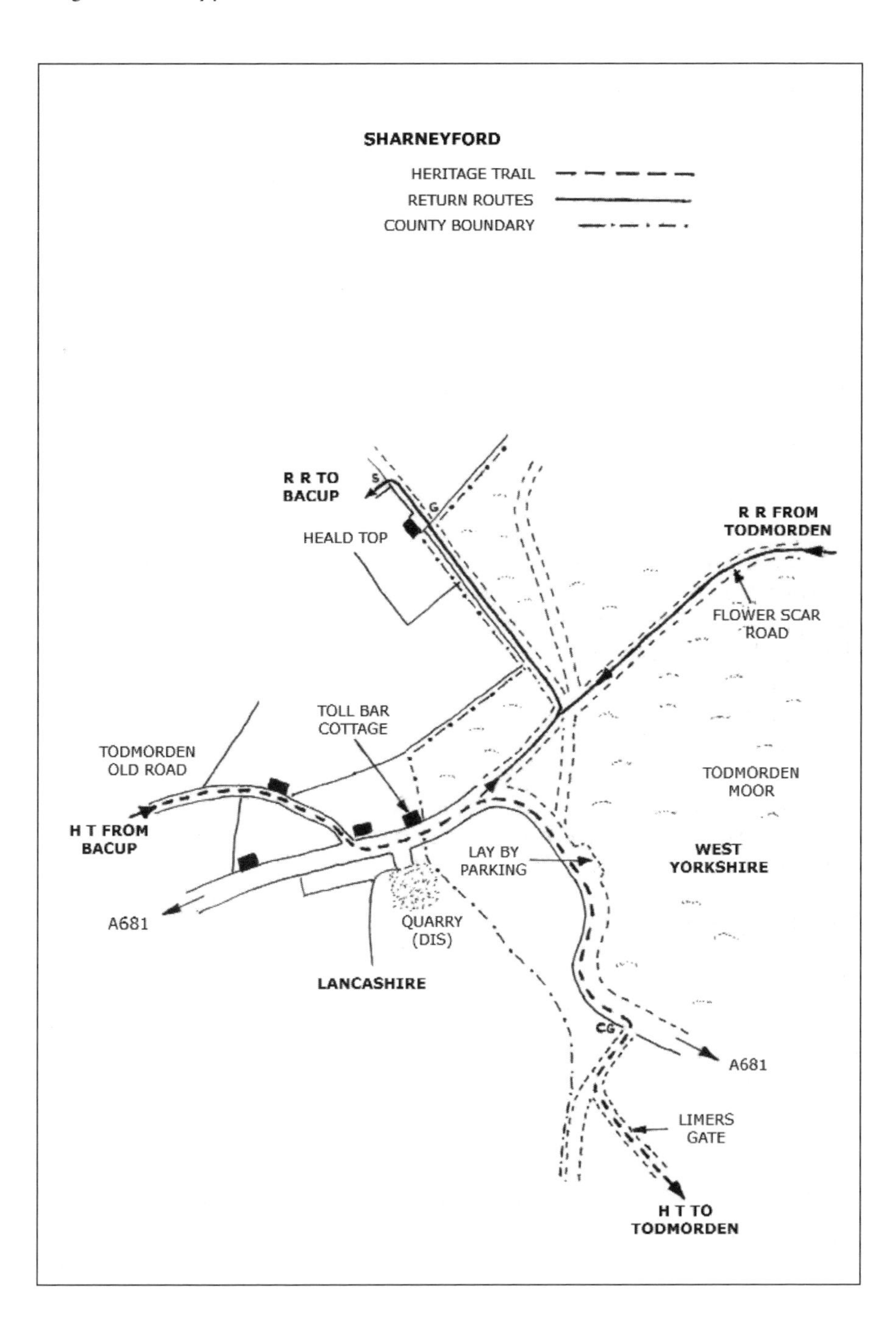
SHARNEYFORD
HERITAGE TRAIL
RETURN ROUTES
COUNTY BOUNDARY
R R TO
BACUP
S
G
HEALD TOP
R R FROM
TODMORDEN
FLOWER SCAR
ROAD
TOLL BAR
COTTAGE
TODMORDEN
OLD ROAD
TODMORDEN
MOOR
H T FROM
BACUP
LAY BY
PARKING
WEST
YORKSHIRE
A681
QUARRY
(DIS)
LANCASHIRE
CG
A681
LIMERS
GATE
H T TO
TODMORDEN

gate and turn left to follow alongside the wall, on top of which are the remnants of an iron fence that is part of the boundary to Dobroyd Castle, seen over to the left. The Victorian, Tudor style castle was built by John Gibson during 1865-1869 for the son of John Fielden MP.

Follow the boundary until reaching a small copse and then negotiate a small gate, to rise up the next pasture with a wooden fence in tandem on the left. Up above is the enviably sited Edge End. Cross the stile, situated 50 metres to the left of the house, and continue up the next field to find a faint indentation angling half-right up to a stone wall. This is a junction of routes, for here we unite with the Calderdale Way. With the wall on the left, continue through three gates to emerge into Parkin Lane. Turn left, and at the first bend (we say farewell to the Calderdale Way), our route continuing ahead, soon passing Stones Lane on the left, after which we take the path on the raised verge on the left side of the lane, from where you have views over upper Calderdale with Bridestones beyond.

Shortly, we arrive at the hamlet of Sourhall and the Sourhall Inn, or is it the Country Friend (this establishment seems to change name on a regular basis but always serves beverages). Go over the cattle-grid or gate to rise up Tower Causeway (lane) with Flower Scar Hill to the left, which is our next objective. The way up is the second track on the left. Climb unfailingly to the top, from where you can see Pendle Hill and the west Pennine moors. There now follows what should be a grand stride of one mile along Flower Scar Road, sadly ruined by scenes of fly tipping. As you descend to the county boundary at Sharneyford, pass beneath transmission lines and then turn left down to the lay-by on the Bacup/Todmorden road (A681) at Sharneyford.

Stage 6: Todmorden to Jack Bridge

Start	Todmorden Town Hall GR 937242
Distance	5 miles (8 km) linear 9.5 miles (15 km) circular
Map	OS Explorer OL21
Parking	Todmorden centre

Leave the roundabout in the centre of Todmorden by following the Railway Station sign up past the White Hart. Continue ahead under the railway viaduct. Now rise up Ridge Steps and turn right along a tarmac walkway through Buckley Wood, from where you have a fine vista of Todmorden Cricket Club and Centre Vale Park. Follow the terraced path to its emergence into Ewood Lane, thence downhill, past the baths and school to the Burnley road (A646). Cross, turn left and after 400 metres, turn right into Stoney Royd Road noting the Calderdale Way sign. On reaching the railway overbridge, turn left, now walking on an enclosed path below the railway embankment.

At the junction, continue ahead. Rise up the lane, soon turning sharp right to pass round East View Barn. Down below, the railway line disappears into Kitson Wood tunnel on its path up to the Cliviger Gorge and Burnley. The track zig-zags up through Kitson Wood, with wonderful views down Cat Hole Clough to the left. On reaching the tree line, pass through the gate with Orchan Rocks ahead. Leave the main track and follow the bridleway signed Stoney Lane, advancing directly up toward the rocks in the company of a wall to the right. At the base of Orchan, turn right to follow the fine bridleway with Lower Hartley Farm on the right. On reaching a junction, turn right into a further bridleway enclosed by walls. There now follows a grand stroll with views over Todmorden to the right and Stoodley Pike ahead, whilst up to the left is Hawk Stones and Bride Stones. On reaching Kit Hill, the Calderdale Way joins from the right. Go through two gates. Ahead now will be Whirlaw Stones, the base of which is gained by a line of causey stones. Pass through the gate where the Calderdale Way continues ahead, but we turn left rising on traces of causeying with Whirlaw Stones on the right.

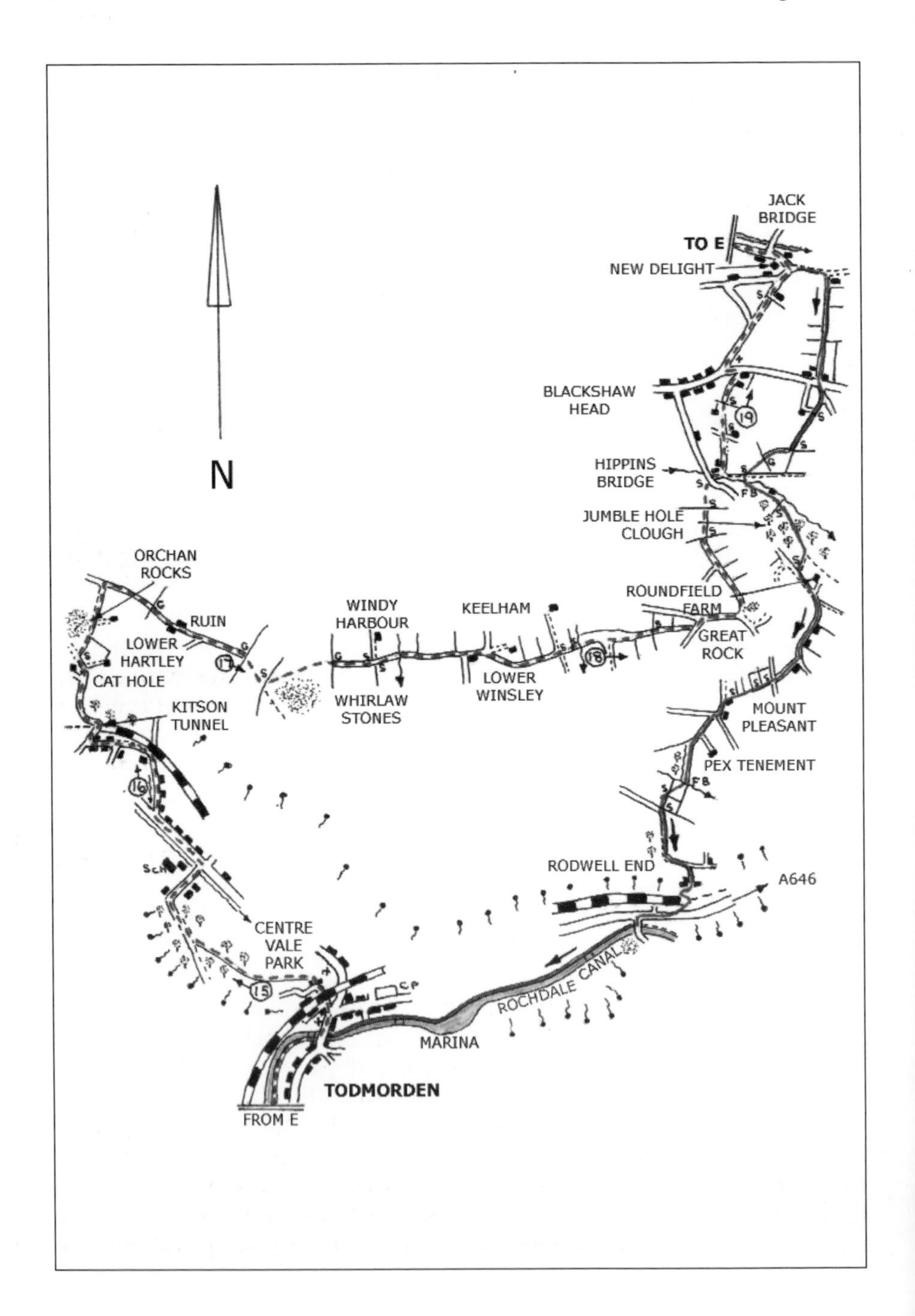

JACK BRIDGE
TO E
NEW DELIGHT
BLACKSHAW HEAD
HIPPINS BRIDGE
JUMBLE HOLE CLOUGH
N
ORCHAN ROCKS
RUIN
LOWER HARTLEY
CAT HOLE
WINDY HARBOUR
KEELHAM
ROUNDFIELD FARM
GREAT ROCK
WHIRLAW STONES
LOWER WINSLEY
KITSON TUNNEL
MOUNT PLEASANT
PEX TENEMENT
RODWELL END
A646
CENTRE VALE PARK
ROCHDALE CANAL
MARINA
TODMORDEN
FROM E

Whirlaw Stones

Cross Whirlaw Common on a grass track to a gate leading into a wall-enclosed bridleway, passing beneath Windy Harbour Farm. The bridleway advances to ford a stream, after which it becomes briefly enclosed, squeezing between high, heather clad bankings. Continue ahead (the way again showing signs of causeystones) to eventually emerge into a vehicular road at Lower Winsley Farm.

Proceed ahead, and when the road turns left uphill, enter the signed, enclosed way on the right, shortly to pass over two stiles situated below Keelham Farm. Follow the obvious path and, soon after crossing a small stream, the Calderdale Way unites with us once more from the right. After two more gates, the path goes forward to a quiet metalled lane. Turn left and then immediately right into Eastwood Road, which leads to Great Rock, where there is a fine view down Calderdale towards Hebden Bridge. Take the walled path to the left of Great Rock that leads onto the edge of Staups Moor. Cross the moor with a wall in tandem on the right. Go over the ladder-stile and descend to the road at Hippings Bridge. Cross the bridge and turn immediately right into the drive at Hippings Farm (hippings is an old description of stepping stones.) Pass to the front of the house, which was built in 1650. (Note the sign on the right for Jumble Hole Clough – if you are contemplating walking the return route, two miles could be saved off the route by taking this link, but you will miss the hospitality of the New Delight Inn! (See map.)

Continue up the track passing the farm buildings to a stile. Rise up to the left of the next farm and cross its access drive onto a paved path with an accompanying wall on the right. Now follow the signed path, avoiding the next farm's yard. Continue along the well defined path, passing through a gate, then bear left into Badger Lane at Blackshaw Head. Turn left, and in 50 metres, turn right into Old Shaw Lane, noting the old milestone which reads 'London – 206 miles'. Stride out along the lane with views of the upper Colden Valley ahead. As you begin to descend, take the bridleway on the right which drops down to the New Delight Inn at Jack Bridge.

New Delight Inn

The Return Route

Jack Bridge to Todmorden

From the doorway of the New Delight Inn, turn right up the road and take the first track on the left, signed Pennine Bridleway. On reaching Shaw Bottom, turn right, again signed Pennine Bridleway, now enclosed by

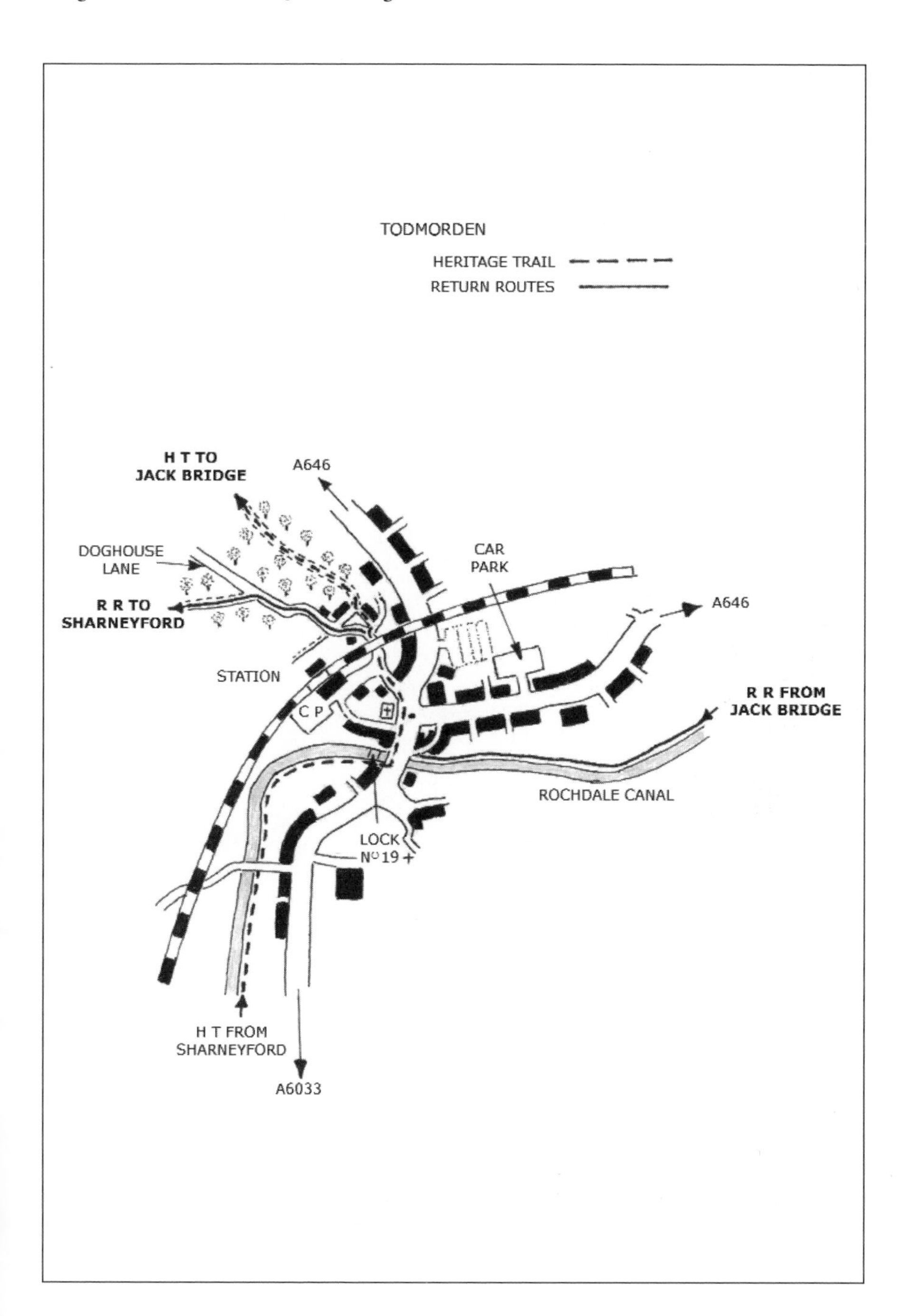
TODMORDEN
HERITAGE TRAIL
RETURN ROUTES
H T TO
JACK BRIDGE
A646
DOGHOUSE
LANE
CAR
PARK
R R TO
SHARNEYFORD
A646
STATION
R R FROM
JACK BRIDGE
C P
ROCHDALE CANAL
LOCK
Nº 19
H T FROM
SHARNEYFORD
A6033

walls. Rise to cross over Pry Hill and then emerge into Badger Lane. Turn left, then immediately right at the bridleway sign. In 40 metres, bear right down the access drive to White Walls Farm. Squeeze through the stile to the left of the farm which sends you into an enclosed way. At its end, go over the stile and turn right to follow the wall round two sides of the field to the gate. Cross to the stile and signpost seen ahead. At this point, you will be joined by anyone who took the link path mentioned earlier. Take the path signed Jumble Hole Clough. Descend the steps and cross the footbridge, noting the rocky bed of the stream. Descend a further flight of steps to arrive at the ruined Staups Mill – a tiny spinning mill in an idyllic setting.

Rise up the leafy way, ignoring the stile on the left, and advance ahead to arrive at a gap-stile. After a short lived section of level walking, the path delves to a junction of paths sited beneath a transmission line. Turn right and ascend up out of the woodland. On the left are the vestiges of a wall over which is the enviably sited Round Field Farm.

Cross over the stile, which leads onto a surfaced track. Turn left and, in 60 metres, the entrance to Round Field Farm goes off to the left, but

Round Field Farm

we advance ahead, where there are great views down Calderdale towards Hebden Bridge. Follow the track round to the right, first passing Hipperholme Farm, then Lane House and Upper House, with its line of ten mullioned windows. Soon you will arrive at Eastwood Lane. Cross to the stile opposite and follow the faintly discernable path, over obvious stiles to eventually pass above, and to the rear of, a row of cottages. Descend the steps into a sunken way. Turn left passing the cottages' gable end and then right to pass in front of Mount Pleasant Cottage. Continue ahead at the junction, into a path enclosed by walls. On the left is Pex Tenements. The path turns left in the company of a stream down to a footbridge, which we cross, and then angles right to rise up to the right hand corner of the field. Go over the stile and follow the wall to Matthew Lane.

Turn left down the lane/track and then right just before the former Rodwell End Chapel to enter the hamlet of Rodwell End, with its manor house, barn and cottages. Leave the hamlet by the path to the left of Rodwell Cottage, which zig-zags steeply down into Calderdale. As you descend, note how the road, canal, railway and river all compete for space in the narrow confines of the valley. The path terminates in a car park and picnic area at the Todmorden/Hebden Bridge road (A646). Turn right along the road and, in 100 metres, cross into Haugh Road and then immediately right onto the towpath of the Rochdale canal, which we follow for 1¼ miles to lock No. 19 at Rochdale Road. Then turn left to the centre of Todmorden.

Todmorden

Situated in the valley of the Calder, Todmorden, meaning 'marshy valley of the foxes', is now wholly in Yorkshire. The fine town hall in the centre of town was originally half in Yorkshire and half in Lancashire, until the county boundaries were altered in the 1940s. The building, constructed in 1875, was designed by John Gibson, who also built the Unitarian Church and Dobroyd Castle (seen on stage 4). Fielden Square, named after local benefactors, is one of the oldest parts of Todmorden.

Town Hall

The Golden Lion Inn, built in the 18th century, was a changing point for horses which hauled the royal mail coach. Todmorden Hall, situated on Rise Lane, is the oldest building in the town, dating from the early 17th century, and standing on the site of an older Radcliffe family building.

The Rochdale Canal

The canal was the first trans-Pennine canal to be constructed, the Act for which was passed in 1794, and was officially opened ten years later, the chief engineer being William Jessop, assisted by William Crossley. In its thirty-three mile journey from Sowerby Bridge to Castlefield in Manchester, it passes through ninety-two locks. Because of the number of locks required to pass through the Pennines, eight reservoirs had to be constructed, one of which is Hollingworth Lake, near Littleborough. The canal was built to accommodate the largest narrow boats, its locks being 74 foot long and 14 foot wide, giving it an enormous thirst for water.

Around the mid 1930s, boats had ceased working along the total length and so, after nearly 150 years, its usage was in decline, finally succumbing to closure in 1952. Locks fell into disrepair and sections became reduced to little more than a watercourse, surrounded by weed and undergrowth, but, worst of all, road overbridges were demolished and the watercourse culverted. Probably the most serious breach was during the construction of the M62 motorway, south of

Gauxholme Lock

Rochdale, where no provisions were made for the canal's reinstatement. However, all was not lost, as in the 1970s, the Rochdale Canal Society was formed and the long task of restoration began. This resulted in the formation of the Rochdale Canal Trust Ltd, with the aim of raising funds for this purpose. After years of hard work and funding, the canal once more became fully navigable, no longer for the conveyance of goods but for the growing numbers of privately owned narrowboats and pleasure craft.

Stage 7: Jack Bridge to New Bridge – Midgehole

Start	Jack Bridge GR 963283
Distance	5.5 miles (8.8 km) linear 7.5 miles (12 km) circular
Map	OS Explorer OL21
Parking	Jack Bridge (roadside)

From the New Delight Inn, descend to Jack Bridge and take the surfaced lane (New Road) on the left, with Colden Water to your right. Note the old Strines Bridge across the fields carrying the ancient route descending from Colden. After passing Lower Strines Farm, the lane curves right to pass in front of Higher Strines. Continue for a further 180 metres to find a stile on the right that sends a faint path showing signs of causeying half-left across the pasture. Go over a stile into a newly planted copse. Advance on the slightly discernable path, but with an accompanying wire fence as a guide. Proceed through a small gate and onto the well maintained Pennine Bridleway.

Turn right, passing Land Farm and Display Gardens, to arrive at Land Bridge, then turn immediately left over the stile. Continue alongside the stream for a mere 20 metres and then turn right. Rise up the path enclosed by a fence and crumbling wall. Soon the footway emerges into Edge Lane at the side of Old Edge Farm, dated 1676. Turn left, where we are once more in the company of the Pennine Bridleway. The lane now becomes unsurfaced, with fine views down to Rodmer Clough and Lord Piece Moor beyond, and then shortly, a glimpse up the remote Noah Dale with its deserted farmstead. On reaching the driveway to Egypt Farm, we continue ahead through the intake gate out onto Standing Stone Hill. Over to the left is the site of the old Reaps Cross on the route over to Raistrick Greave and Gorple. Continue up the well defined bridleway, soon cresting the ridge with magnificent views. Directly ahead is the Packhorse Inn (or the Ridge), beyond which are the Walshaw reservoirs, which are on the route of the Pennine Way to Top Withins and, below, Lower Gorple

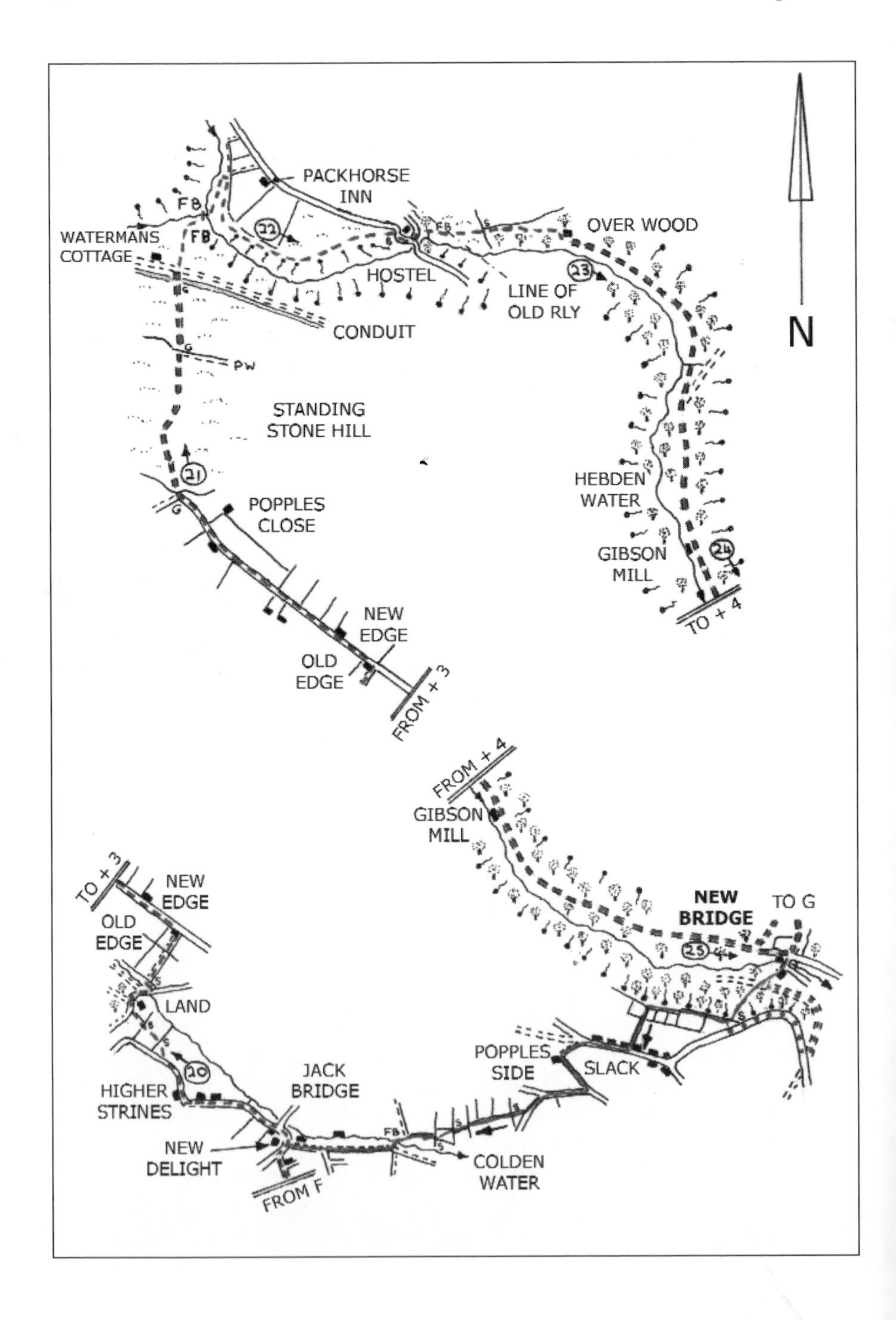
PACKHORSE
INN
FB
FB
WATERMANS
COTTAGE
22
HOSTEL
OVER WOOD
23
LINE OF
OLD RLY
CONDUIT
N
PW
STANDING
STONE HILL
21
HEBDEN
WATER
POPPLES
CLOSE
GIBSON
MILL
24
TO + 4
NEW
EDGE
OLD
EDGE
FROM + 3
FROM + 4
GIBSON
MILL
TO + 3
NEW
EDGE
OLD
EDGE
NEW
BRIDGE
TO G
25
LAND
20
POPPLES
SIDE
SLACK
HIGHER
STRINES
JACK
BRIDGE
FB
NEW
DELIGHT
COLDEN
WATER
FROM F

reservoir and the waterman's house. To the left is Black Hameldon, then the Gorple Gap and in the north-west, Lad Law.

Descend now, soon arriving at a gate and stile, at which point we are joined by the Pennine Way, which comes in from the right. Continue ahead to the next wrought iron gate. Pass over the catchment drain and the access track to the waterman's house at Lower Gorple.

Continue to descend, but now on a roughly paved causey-stoned way to the meeting of Reaps Water and Graining Water. Cross the two footbridges, turning left to ascend the paved footway with Graining down to the left. When a direction post is met, it's decision time! The Heritage Trail turns back sharp right. If you require refreshment, continue ahead for 10 metres and then go right over the stile, which leads up the field to Widdop Road and the Packhorse Inn (open daily but only between Easter and October). After turning sharp right, continue along the edge of the valley of Graining Water in the company of a crumbling wall to your left. It's a fine stride passing between rock and bracken, gradually descending to a gate and steps (missing), to emerge into the roadway opposite the Scouts hostel at Blake Dean. The building was originally the Baptist Chapel (note the graveyard to the side). Continue down to Blake Dean Bridge, do not cross, but turn left into the enclosed track and in 30 metres

New Bridge Hall

go through the gate on the right and descend the steps to the footbridge over Alcomden Water.

Climb the pathway, including stone steps, and cross a level trackway, which is the trackbed of an old railway route used in the construction of the Walshaw Dean reservoirs. (If you walk down the route of the line for 100 metres, you can look down onto the remains of the piers that carried the bridge over the valley.) Retrace your steps to continue up the inclined path onto the moor and follow the way, unerringly, to the entrance of Overwood Plantation. Descend to pass to the front of Overwood Cottages and continue down the access drive under an umbrella of trees. After 1000 metres, join the main estate road down Hebden Valley. On reaching Gibson Mill, you can leave the estate road and follow Hebden Water down to the lodge at New Bridge. The estate road continues directly ahead down to the entrance lodge.

The Return Route

New Bridge / Slack / Jack Bridge

From the Lodge, descend and then turn right to cross New Bridge. Continue ahead with New Bridge Hall to your left and rise up the stony track to reach a tarmac road. At this point, it's decision time again – softies should turn left up the road until meeting the Calderdale Way. Turn right and follow this up to the Hebden/Slack road where we turn right (no footway). Pass Lee Bank on the left, then over the stile on the right where the toughies will be waiting! Toughies will cross over the tarmac road and climb up through the trees. As the path steepens, your toils are eased by an occasional flight of steps. On nearing the rim of the escarpment, the final steps are built of natural stone and, after leaf fall or ice, can become treacherous! Go over the stile into pastureland where the softies will be waiting!!

Turn right along the escarpment – first in the pastures and then over a stone step-stile with the fence on the left. Shortly, a post bearing a yellow top-marker will be met. Turn left here away from the scarp. Cross a small, rough field and advance into a wall-enclosed track which emerges into the roadway at Slack. Cross the road and turn right. Continue along the wide verge. Ignore the road turning right to Widdop and Colne. Pass the entrance to High Court and then take the next left onto Popples Common. On reaching the cottages at Popples Side, a sign sends a briefly enclosed path between the buildings, where views now open up looking down Colden Clough toward its junction with Calderdale and the hamlet of

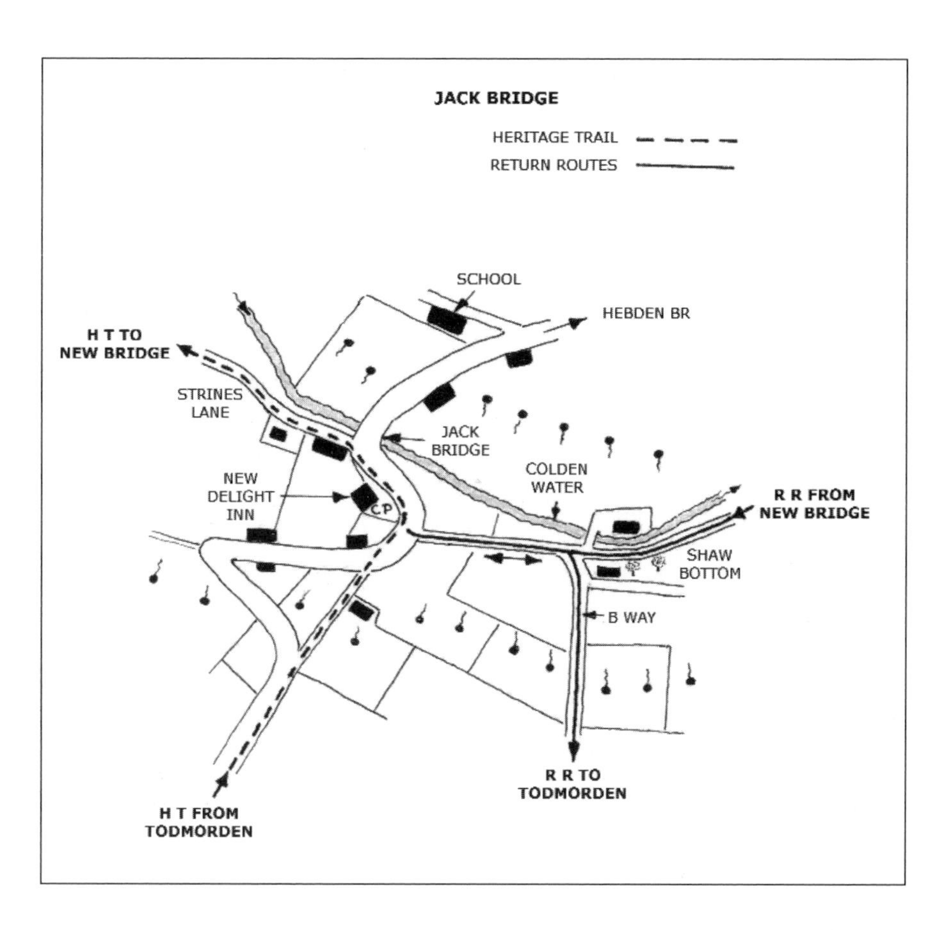

Mytholm. Turn sharp right at the next junction onto a fine stone flag path, which is part of the Caderdale Way, then turn left at the next junction, signed Colden Clough. In 100 metres go right (signed CW), passing above a small copse planted around 1990. Follow the obvious path which once more becomes paved.

Pass through stiles, crossing the final field diagonally, still on pavings, into the top corner of Foster Wood. Go along the top of the wood where soon the Pennine Way comes in from the right to join us. Descend and cross Colden Water via Hebble Hole bridge (clapper bridge). Once across, turn right and rise up the bank onto a track. Turn right, passing Hudson Mill, built in 1738, now converted into a private residence. Continue ahead to arrive back at Jack Bridge.

Hardcastle Craggs / Hebden Valley

Thousands of people visit Hardcastle Crags in the Hebden valley to picnic by the river or simply to walk the miles of footpaths. Much of the valley is owned by the National Trust and contains a nature trail – the Slurring Rock, which begins at the entrance lodge car park (booklet available).The craggs are two large rocky mounds half way up the valley and have given their name to the whole area.

Hidden in the heart of the valley is Gibson Mill and a group of cottages, built around 1800. Initially water powered, the mill was converted to steam in 1860, and closed down at the turn of the century. Higher up the valley are the stone bases of a huge wooden trestle bridge which was built in 1900 to carry a narrow gauge railway, which ran from a shanty town near Heptonstall to the site of the Walshaw Dean reservoirs. The bridge was 105 feet high and 700 feet in length and was demolished when construction of the reservoirs was completed in 1912.

Stage 8: New Bridge – Midgehole to Grain Water Bridge

Start	New Bridge GR 982292
Distance	2.5 miles (4 km) linear 4.5 miles (7.25 km) circular
Map	OS Explorer OL21
Parking	New Bridge (charge)

Leave New Bridge by taking the estate road signed Top Car Park. Rise up the tarmac lane. In 200 metres, at the edge of the wood and aforementioned car park, turn left and in 100 metres go right into the enclosed path, paved with causey stones. Follow the old route unfailingly, first between pastures and then angling left to rise up through Foul Scout Wood to arrive at Slurring Rock on the edge of the escarpment. Ignore the path going off to the left, but follow the causey stones and accompanying wall, shortly turning right to pass over a stile, which directs you up an enclosed path between vestiges of walls, soon to emerge into the hamlet of Shackleton.

There are lovely views down into the valley of Hebden Water, with the villages of Heptonstall and Slack beyond. Turn right into Shackleton and take the signed path on the left, which passes between barn and cottages. Pass over the stile into pastureland with a wall for company to the right. Pass through a gap and aim for the two gates seen ahead, taking the one on the right. The boundary fence will now be on the left and, as you stride along, you can admire the excellent views of Crimsworth Dean down to the right, with the two Brown Knolls beyond. After passing through a small gate, the fence is now to your right. Follow this along to Abel Cote Farm. Pass in front of the house and left round the barn turning right onto the access track. Soon you will arrive at Abel Cross, a double cross of medieval times situated on the line of an ancient route.

Continue down to a junction and turn left, soon passing Laithe Farm on the right. A further 500 metres brings you to a junction of tracks at the derelict Nook Farm. The cross track coming in from the left is Limers

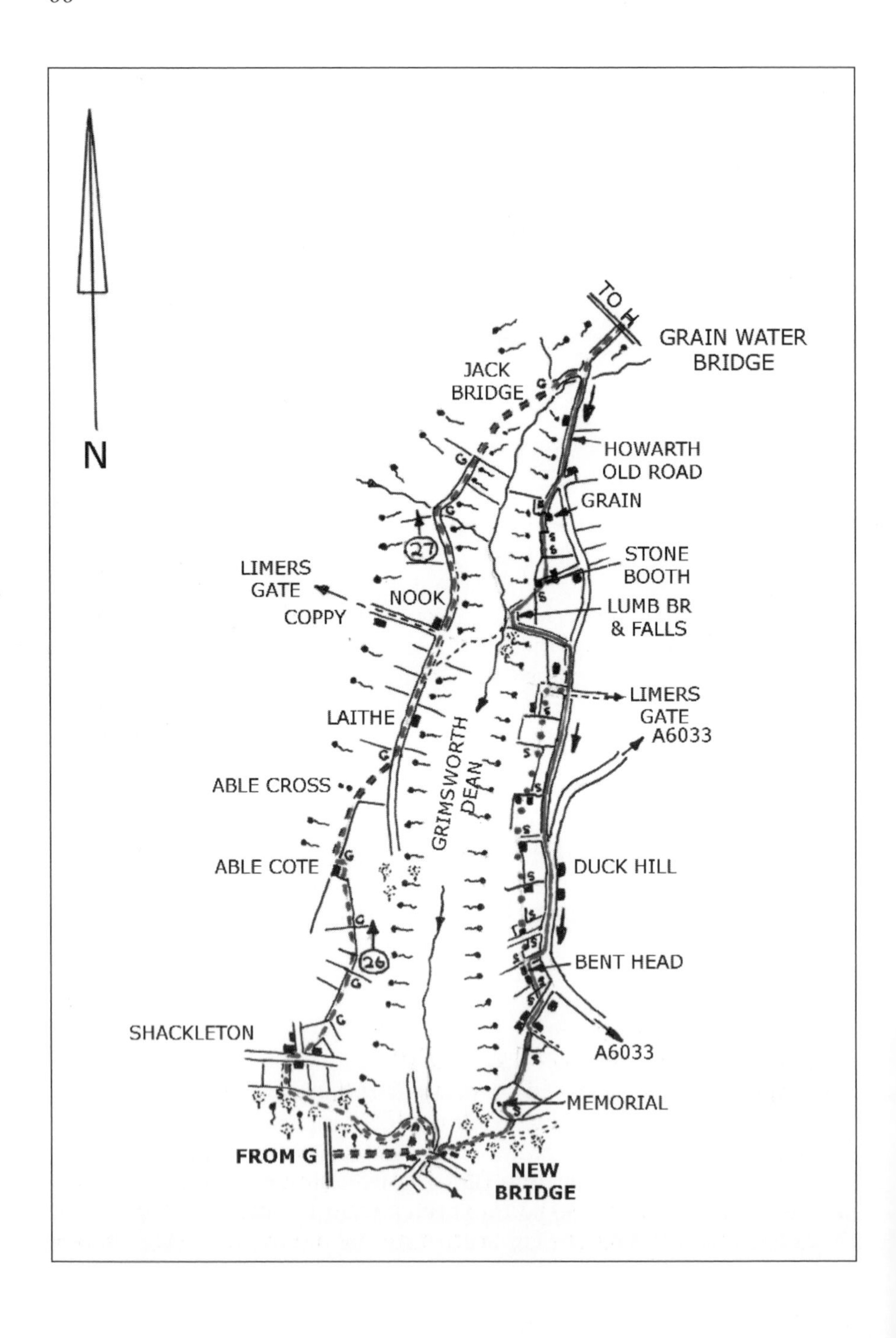
N
TO H
GRAIN WATER BRIDGE
JACK BRIDGE
HOWARTH OLD ROAD
GRAIN
27
STONE BOOTH
LIMERS GATE
NOOK
COPPY
LUMB BR & FALLS
LIMERS GATE
A6033
LAITHE
GRIMSWORTH DEAN
ABLE CROSS
ABLE COTE
DUCK HILL
26
BENT HEAD
SHACKLETON
A6033
MEMORIAL
FROM G
NEW BRIDGE

Abel Cross

Gate, on its way from Lancashire by way of Widdop and Walshaw. Dropping down to cross Crimsworth Dean Beck at Lumb Bridge, it then climbs over Flaight Hill and High Brown Knoll on its way to Luddenden and Halifax.

Continue ahead on a fine stride, passing the remains of Baby House Farm and then descend to the bridge, spanning Paddock Beck. Pass through a gate to accompany Grain Water up to Grain Water Bridge at Howarth Old Road.

The Return Route

Grain Water Bridge to New Bridge

Turn right along Howarth Old Road, crossing the bridge and soon passing Greystones on the right. Now continue for a further 300 metres before turning right down the driveway to Grain Farm. Pass between the barn and the 16th century farmhouse to find a small gate giving access into the pasture. Turn left, with a wall to your left and, in 120 metres, cross a stone step-stile into the higher field. Turn right to follow the yellow marker

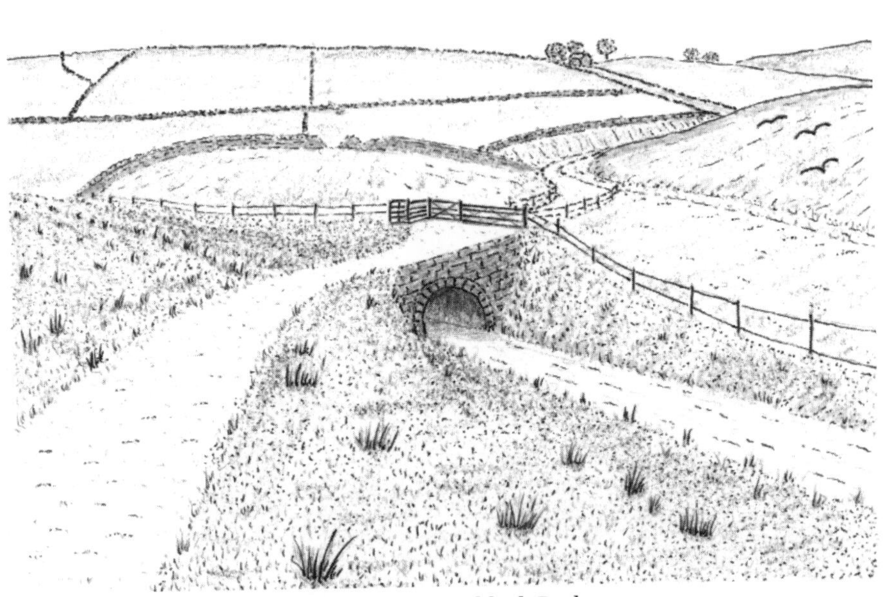

Bridge over Paddock Beck

posts, which will direct you across two fields to a stile on the lower side of the barn at Stone Booth Farm. The Way is arrowed through the yard, passing in front of the farmhouse to a squeeze-stile. This sends a faint path that angles slightly to a second stile. Now descend the field to enter an enclosed path between a wall and fence. Turn left to arrive at Lumb Bridge and Falls, a delectable place where the ancient bridge carries the old Limers Gate over Crimsworth Dean Beck with the falls just below.

After lingering awhile, do not cross the bridge, but take the path to the left of the waterfall, which crosses a second flagged bridge over a sidestream. A sharp left turn sends you up the steep, enclosed section of Limers Gate, which at first is well paved but becomes slightly damp as you gain height. At the top, turn right to emerge into Howarth Old Road. Pass Gib Farm on the right, soon reaching the driveway to Barker Cote, also on the right. At this point, you have a choice of routes. The alternative continues along Howarth Old Road to rejoin the main route at Bent Head. This route gives stile-free walking along a quiet road with views over Crimsworth Dean (see map). The main route turns right down the drive to Barker Cote. Do not enter the yard but take the stile on the left into

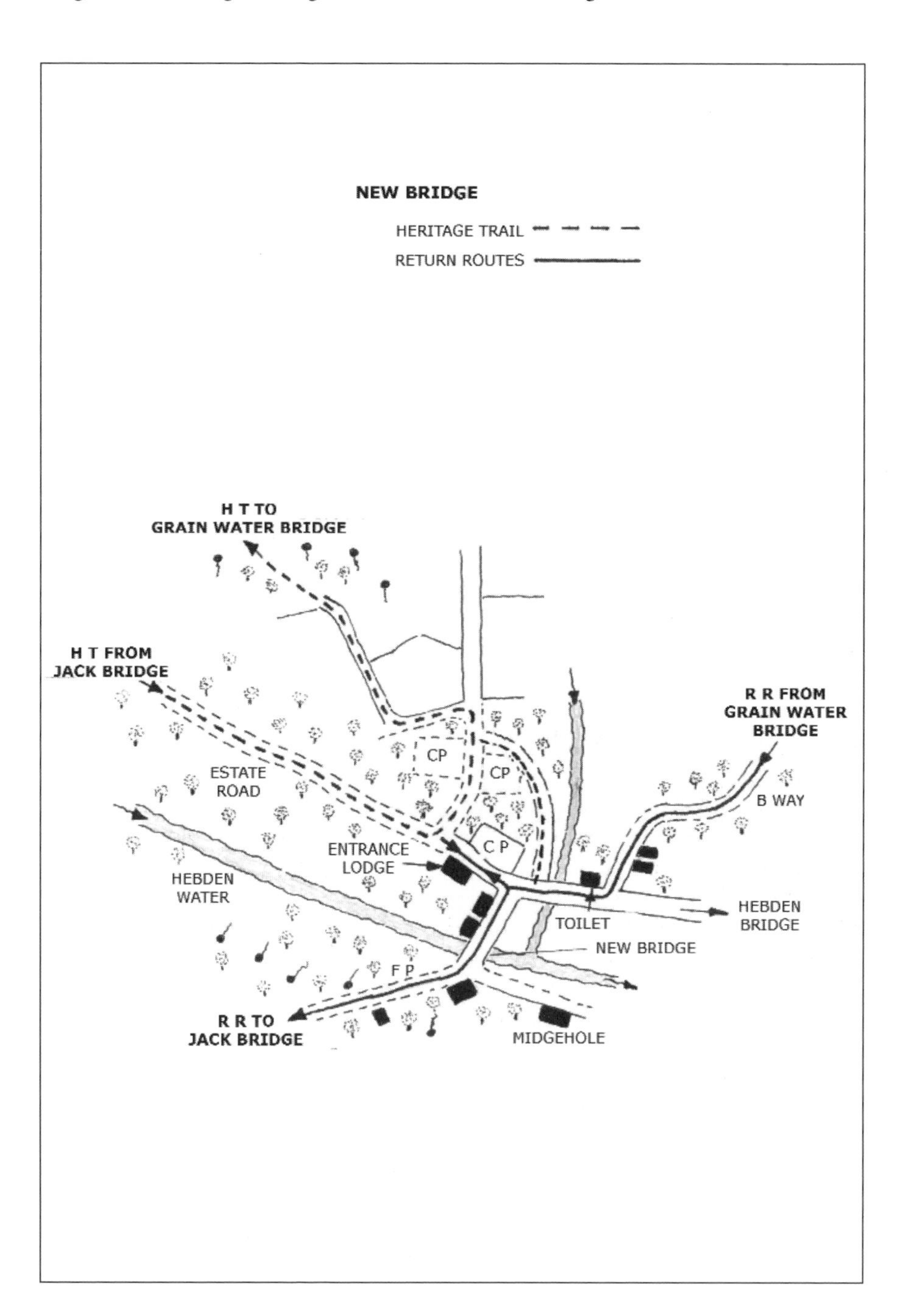
NEW BRIDGE
HERITAGE TRAIL
RETURN ROUTES
H T TO
GRAIN WATER BRIDGE
H T FROM
JACK BRIDGE
R R FROM
GRAIN WATER
BRIDGE
CP
CP
C P
ESTATE
ROAD
B WAY
ENTRANCE
LODGE
HEBDEN
WATER
TOILET
HEBDEN
BRIDGE
NEW BRIDGE
F P
R R TO
JACK BRIDGE
MIDGEHOLE

the field and turn right to pass the house. There now follows a succession of seven farmhouses, all built on the same contour, some of which have records dating back 500 years. The path is quite obvious (follow the map), passing over numerous stiles. On reaching Bent Head, the alternative route comes in from the left.

Walk through the cobbled yard with the house on your right. Pass into the field via a metal gate. Now follow the right hand boundary to a stile, which leads into the access drive to Lower Crimsworth Farm and Cottages. Turn right. On reaching the hamlet, turn left, then immediately right into a tightly enclosed footway. This in turn sends a path across the pasture to the War Memorial on Smeekin Hill. Similar in design to Stoodley Pike, though on a smaller scale, the memorial commemorates the 1914-18 war. Keeping to the left of the structure, follow the path down towards Pecket Clough. On reaching a stile, turn right down into woodland, with the vestiges of a wall to your left, to merge onto Ray Gate. The ancient packhorse route winds its way downhill to finally emerge into Midgehole Road. Turn right to The Lodge and car parks at New Bridge.

Stage 9: Grain Water Bridge to Oxenhope

Start	Grain Water Bridge GR 996824
Distance	3 miles (4.8 km) linear 6 miles (9.6 km) circular
Map	OS Explorer OL21
Parking	Grain Water Bridge (roadside)

From Grain Water, rise steeply up the tarmaced Howarth Old Road to pass Lane Head Barn on the right and then the access drive to Thurrish Farm going off to the left. At this point the old road ceases to be surfaced.

Boundary Stone

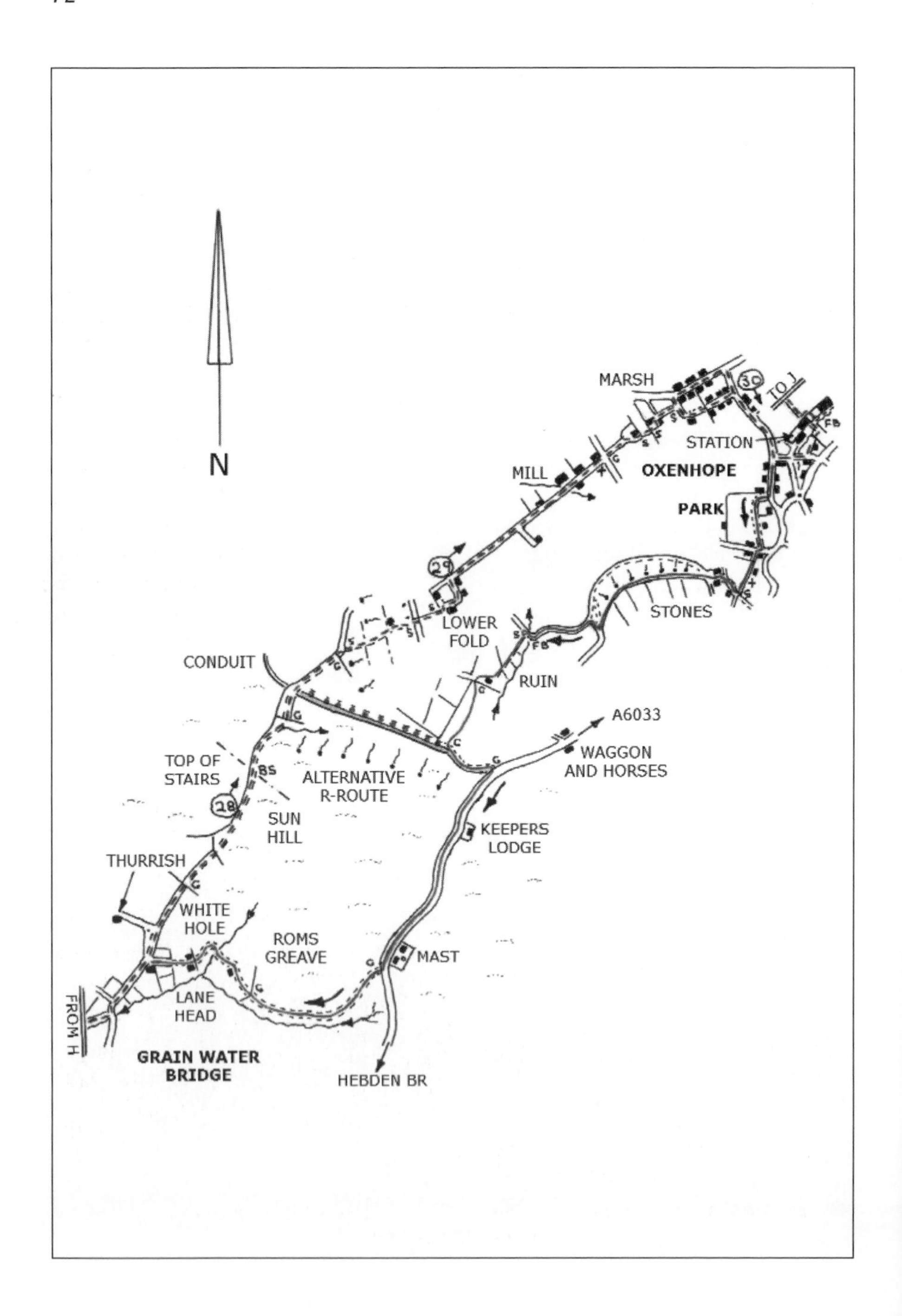
N
MARSH
30
TO J
FB
STATION
MILL
OXENHOPE
PARK
29
LOWER
FOLD
STONES
CONDUIT
FB
RUIN
A6033
WAGGON
AND HORSES
TOP OF
STAIRS
BS
ALTERNATIVE
R-ROUTE
28
SUN
HILL
KEEPERS
LODGE
THURRISH
WHITE
HOLE
ROMS
GREAVE
MAST
LANE
HEAD
FROM H
GRAIN WATER
BRIDGE
HEBDEN BR

Climb gradually to reach the summit at Top o'th Stairs where there is a boundary stone with a bench mark and the letters O.M. Over to the right, the masts on the A6033 at Cock Hill will be visible and, as the route starts to descend, Oxenhope and the valley of Bridgehouse Beck come into view. After passing through a gate on the edge of Sun Hill Clough, a signpost will be met on the right pointing along a catchwater conduit (you will arrive back at this point if you take one of the return routes).

Continue down Stairs Lane. On passing through a second gate, go up the banking on the right to negotiate the squeeze-stile, which sends a slightly discernable path angling over to the right hand boundary. Follow the crumbling walls down, keeping to the right of a ruined farm. Go ahead, through a line of waterworks boundary stones, to find a stile at the corner of a subsantial stone wall and then a stone step-stile. Now with a fence on your left, proceed down to the stile at the corner of the field at Lower Fold Farm. Turn right into the access drive, which is followed left, then right into Outside Lane. Over on the left is Leeshaw Reservoir and, ahead, Penistone Hill and Brontë country. Pass a mill on the left and then rise up to the Baptist Sabbath School, dated 1832, situated at the junction with Moorside Lane. Go directly across into the track signed Marsh and, after

Oxenhope Station

250 metres, enter the yard. Keep to the right of the house to enter a briefly enclosed path which leads out into a small field. Cross on vestiges of causeying to the next group of buildings. Go over a stile into a flagged, hand-railed walkway and then turn left up by the barn, then right into a tightly enclosed footway. Advance through a kissing-gate into a short-lived, enclosed way to emerge onto an access drive with a post signed Millennium Way. You could turn right here to pass by Hoylesyke Farm and down to The Croft, to arrive at Moorhouse Lane, but this is not officially the right of way, so turn left, and then right by the Wesleyan Sunday School, dated 1836, to enter the hamlet of Marsh. Continue along Marsh Lane and then first right down Moorhouse Lane. After 150 metres, pass The Croft on the right, mentioned earlier. Continue to descend Moorhouse Lane, turning left into Mill Lane and arrive at Oxenhope station on the Keighley and Worth Valley Railway.

The Return Route

Oxenhope station to Grain Water Bridge

From the station, turn right into Mill Lane and then first left up Cross Lane. When the lane narrows, turn right to pass below the school playground. Advance up through the park, on the obvious path, to reach the entrance gates. Turn right down Shaw Lane for 75 metres to take the signed path on the left. Rise up the briefly enclosed path to a kissing gate, which directs you up the pasture with Oxenhope church, dedicated to St. Mary the Virgin, on the left. Pass through a second kissing gate, turning right into a driveway. Keep to the right of the cottage and enter a tightly enclosed footway. Pass Old Croft Cottage to meet a junction of ways. Continue ahead, taking the higher path with a stone wall on the left along Top of Stones. This is a delectable stride along the gritstone heather clad outcrop, with views over Oxenhope and the moors above Howarth beyond.

As the path starts to descend, turn sharp right and, after 50 metres, go left on a barely discernable path, which drops down to join a bridleway below. Turn left into the enclosed way that is followed until reaching a planked footbridge at Rag Clough Beck. Cross and then turn back left to pass over a second footbridge and over a stile marked Millennium Way. Rise up the fields, with a crumbling wall to the right, to gain the ruined farmhouse. Pass to the right of the buildings and then ascend to the old intake gate, adjacent to the waterworks catchment channel. Advance through the gate onto rough moorland but now on a well defined track,

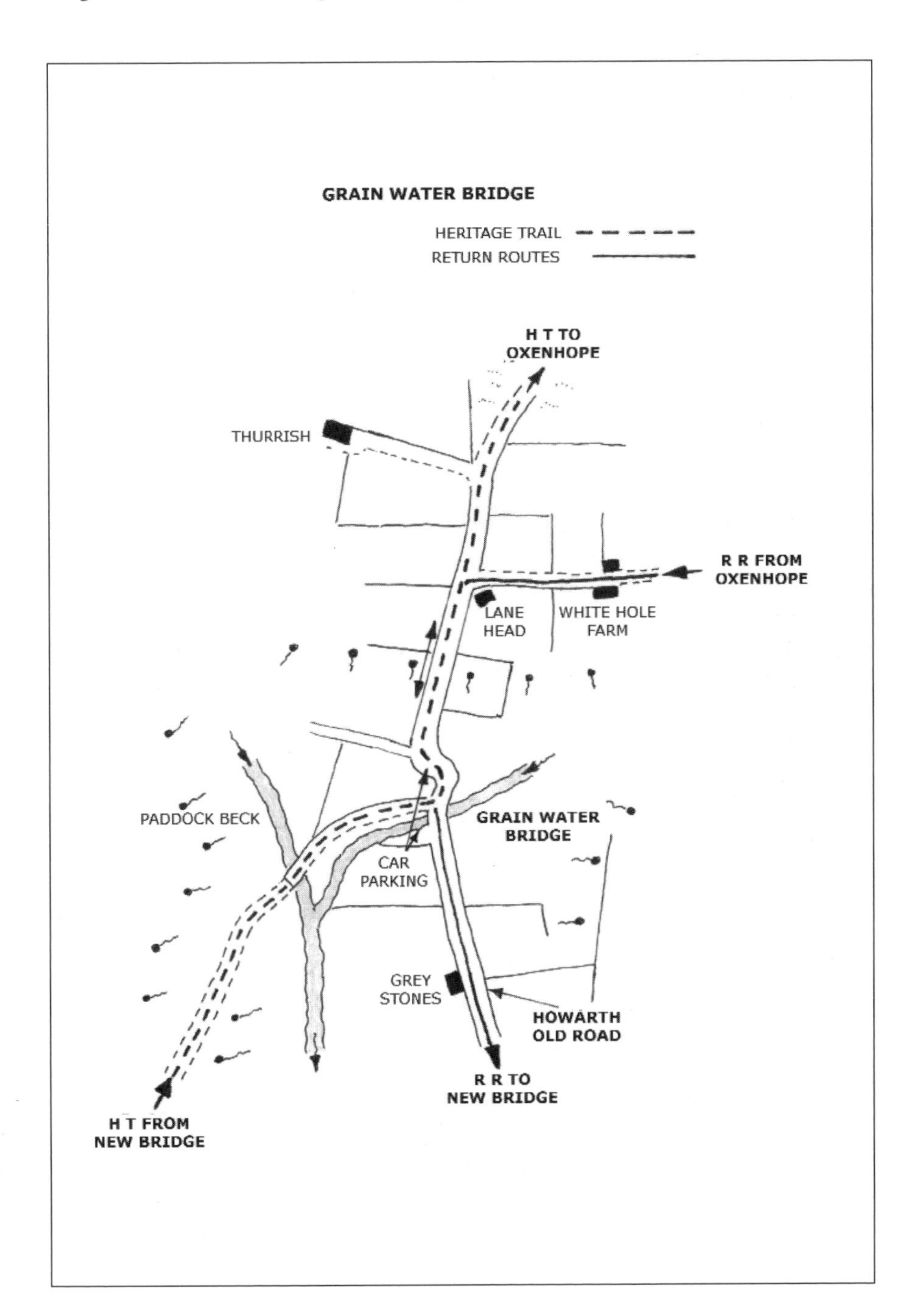
GRAIN WATER BRIDGE
HERITAGE TRAIL
RETURN ROUTES
H T TO
OXENHOPE
THURRISH
R R FROM
OXENHOPE
LANE
HEAD
WHITE HOLE
FARM
PADDOCK BECK
GRAIN WATER
BRIDGE
CAR
PARKING
GREY
STONES
HOWARTH
OLD ROAD
R R TO
NEW BRIDGE
H T FROM
NEW BRIDGE

which is followed up to a second channel. At this point, it's decision time. If there are children in your party, it is advisable to turn right and follow the catchment channel to its junction with Howarth Old Road, and then turn left to follow the outward route over Top of Stairs and back down to Grain Water Bridge.

The alternative turns left to follow the catchment channel to the Hebden Bridge road (A6033) and turn right. There now follows half a mile of road walking (no footway). Pass Keepers Cottage on the left and then the boundary stone at the summit of Cockhill, with its paraphernalia of masts. In 20 metres, turn right at the Bridleway sign. Follow the track as it descends into Roms Clough, with a transmission line and stream for company. After half a mile, the intake gate will be reached. The Way now continues downhill, passing Roms Greave Barn, and then crosses Red Dike Beck to gain White Hole Farm. The route passes to the rear of the farmhouse and continues ahead down the access road to the junction with Howarth Old Road at Lane Head Barn that dates from the 18th century. Turn left and drop steeply down the lane to regain Grain Water Bridge.

Stage 10: Oxenhope station to Oakworth station (KWVR)

Start	Oxenhope station GR 033354
Distance	3 miles (4.8 km) linear 6 miles (9.6 km) circular
Map	OS Explorer OL21
Parking	Overflow car park (Mill Lane)

Turn left out of the station entrance into Mill Lane. Cross over the beck and then turn left. The overflow car park is now on the left and on the right is a cottage dated 1823. Continue ahead, with Bridgehouse Beck and the railway carriage shed alongside. Cross over the footbridge and up onto the railway. Stop, look and listen before crossing, and go up the incline to a stile in the boundary wall. Rise up the pasture, keeping to the wall side to gain the yard at Bents House, which was 'Three Chimneys' in the *The Railway Children* film. Leave via the access drive that merges into Marsh Lane. Turn to the left and, after 100 metres, go right up Old Oxenhope Lane, passing Old Oxenhope Hall on the left. When the lane bends, turn right into the yard at Old Oxenhope Farm and then take the signed path to Howarth, which follows the wall side on the left, over which is a small pond. After passing through two stiles, the path becomes tightly enclosed for a short distance, we then continue ahead with a wall to the right. Pass over a stile into a second enclosed section with Hole Farm down to the right. Cross over its access drive and follow on across two pastures towards Snowden's Farm. On reaching the field corner, turn right into a tightly enclosed footway that descends and zig-zags to pass above Howarth car park. Proceed ahead, now on pavings, to a metal kissing gate that gives access to the churchyard. The Brontë Parsonage is up to the left now and St. Michael's parish church is on the right.

Turn right to pass the Kings Arms and into the cobbled main street. Pass the entrance door to the Tourist Information Centre, and turn left into Changegate. At its end, turn right and then cross into Mytholmes Lane. After 70 metres, turn right and descend South View to find a

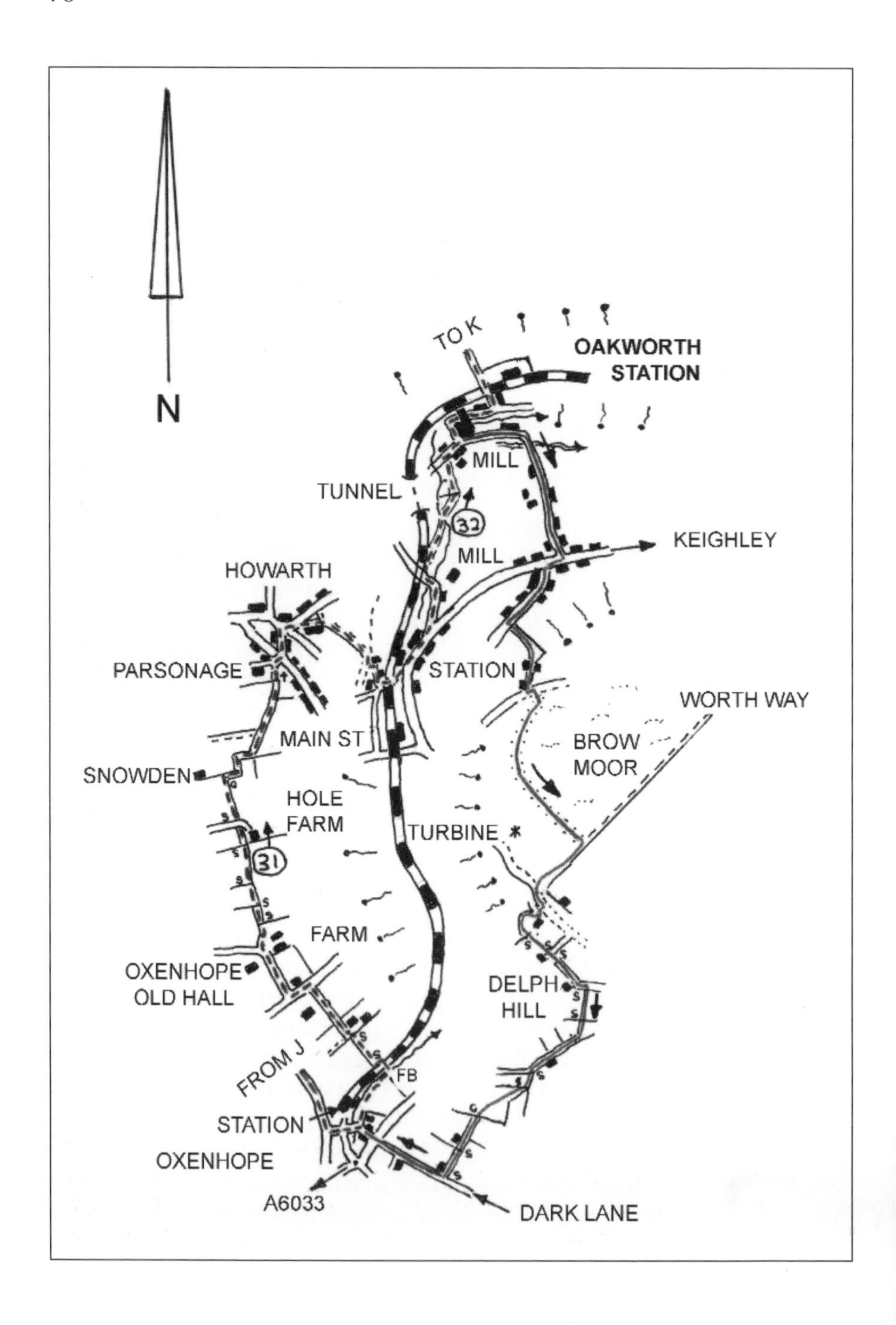
N
TO K
OAKWORTH
STATION
MILL
TUNNEL
32
KEIGHLEY
MILL
HOWARTH
PARSONAGE
STATION
WORTH WAY
MAIN ST
BROW
MOOR
SNOWDEN
HOLE
FARM
TURBINE
31
FARM
OXENHOPE
OLD HALL
DELPH
HILL
FROM J
FB
STATION
OXENHOPE
A6033
DARK LANE

Brontë Parsonage

squeeze stile leading onto a surfaced path. Turn right and follow this downhill with an accompanying wall to the right. Ahead is the eastern side of Howarth, topped by Brow Moor. When the surfaced path ends, turn right, then keep left to go round the white painted Mill Hill Farm. Now turn right to descend to Belle Isle road, then left to cross the footbridge over the KWVR. to gain Howarth station. From the station forcourt, turn left and proceed along Mill Hey for 400 metres, then go left to descend Ebor Lane and cross Bridgehouse Beck via the footbridge. Immediately cross the lane and enter the signed, leafy, enclosed path which at first runs alongside the railway. Note the southern portal of Mytholmes tunnel ahead as the Way turns right, to recross Bridgehouse Beck once more. Follow the obvious path to eventually arrive at a stile onto Mytholmes Lane. Turn right to pass Vale Fold Cottages, soon meeting a junction with Vale Mill Lane. (The Heritage Trail turns left here towards Oakworth station. Anyone walking the return route to Oxenhope should turn right, a description of which follows. See map.) After turning left, walk down

The long lost Standard Class 4 MT 2-6-4 No. 80091

Station Road and cross over the River Worth. Take care here on the blind bend. The KWVR is now up to the left. Pass beneath the disused mill buildings via the underpass, after which the road turns left to arrive at Oakworth station.

Return Route

Oakworth station to Oxenhope

Retrace the route back to the Mytholmes Lane junction. Follow Vale Mill Lane uphill, with no footway at first. As the route bends right, great views of the Keighley and Worth Valley Railway will be seen as it makes its way down the Worth valley. Continue up the lane to its junction with the Howarth/Keighley road, where a right turn brings a second junction. Take the way signed Oxenhope and Hebden Bridge. Follow Hebden Road for approximately 400 metres to find a signed path on the left. Ascend the wall-enclosed path, which soon angles right up to Brow Top Barn and pause here to admire the view across to Howarth and Brontë country. Go through the gate and pass between the buildings. Now turn left up to Brow Top Farm yard and then out onto Brow Top Road.

Turn left and, in a few metres, go right at the footpath sign, which sends a faint path up onto Brow Moor. Ignore the path going off to the right, but continue ahead to meet a well-defined track, turning right onto this. Follow the way across the heather clad moor, with the wind turbine to the right on the edge of Brow Moor. On reaching a stone wall, turn right to join forces with the Worth Way. The path now descends to Black Moor

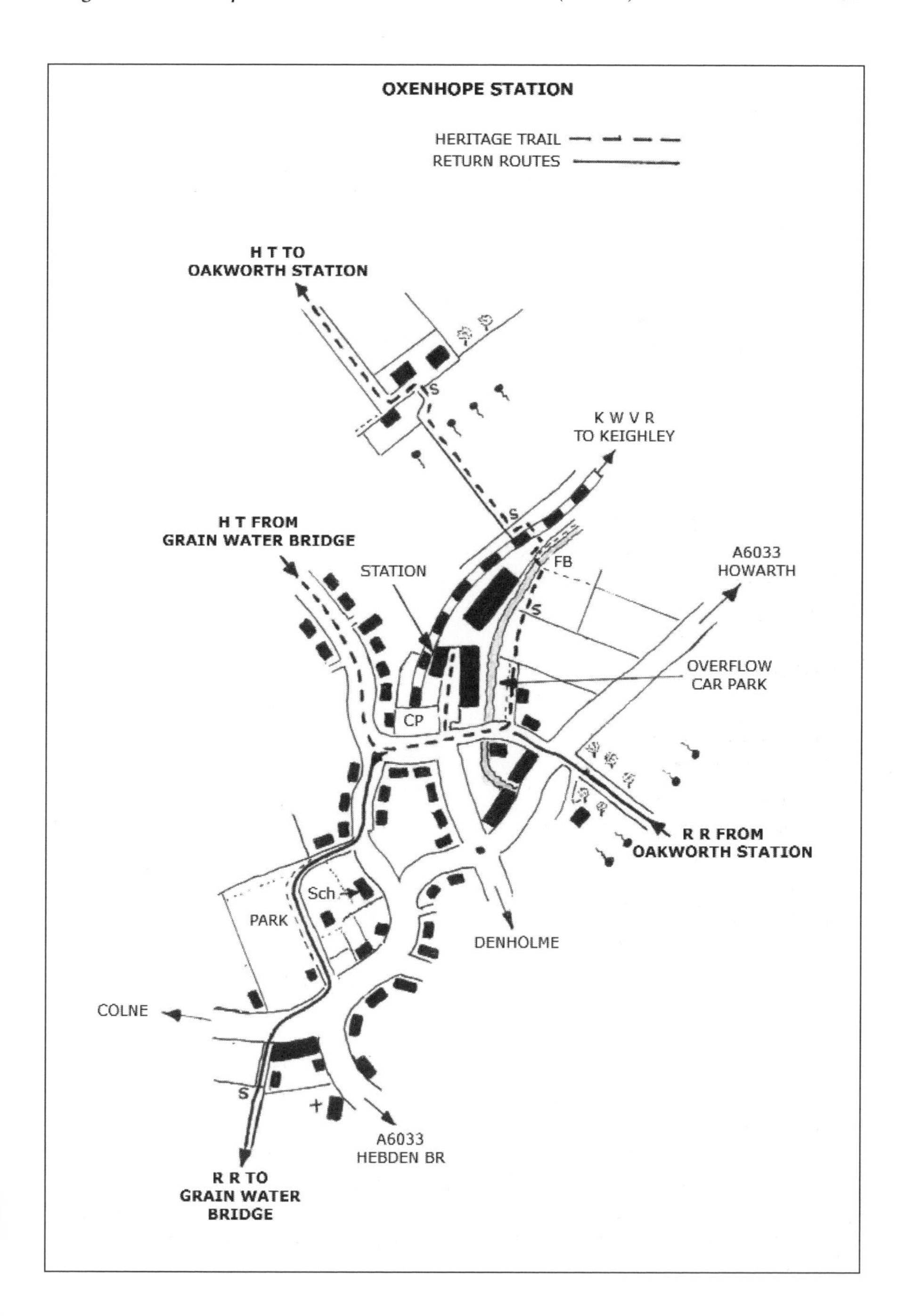
OXENHOPE STATION
HERITAGE TRAIL
RETURN ROUTES
H T TO
OAKWORTH STATION
S
K W V R
TO KEIGHLEY
H T FROM
GRAIN WATER BRIDGE
S
STATION
FB
A6033
HOWARTH
S
OVERFLOW
CAR PARK
CP
R R FROM
OAKWORTH STATION
Sch
PARK
DENHOLME
COLNE
S
A6033
HEBDEN BR
R R TO
GRAIN WATER
BRIDGE

Lane where a left turn is made. In 30 metres, turn right at a Worth Way sign. Descend to a stile and steps that lead onto the driveway to Lower Nailer Hill and Duck Cottage. Proceed past the cottage, turning left round the gable end. Now follow the waymarked path, which angles right to a squeeze-stile and turns left to follow the wall to an access drive to the enviably situated Upper Royd House Farm. Go directly across and advance along the charming pathway. On reaching Delph Hill Farm, continue ahead up its driveway for 60 metres to find a Worth Way sign hidden on the right. Pass over and follow the obvious path across two fields to a stile and gate leading into a walled green lane that leads down to pass into a farmyard. Continue ahead down the surfaced drive until a sign reading 'No Footpath' is met. Follow the Worth Way sign going off to the left. The route keeps to the left hand boundary and then over a stile in the field corner. Now angle half right towards a gate seen ahead with a broken step-stile to its left. These lead into a walled, enclosed track which is followed to Lower Hayley. Advance ahead through two gates followed by the world's smallest gap-stile! This sends the route along a briefly enclosed path leading into Dark Lane. Turn right and descend to the Hebden/Keighley road. Cross into Harry Lane, where the overflow car park is on the right, and continue ahead on Mill Lane to Oxenhope station.

The Keighley and Worth Valley Railway

British Rail ran its last passenger train up the Worth valley branch line in late 1961-96 years after its construction. In 1962, an inaugural meeting with the goal of re-opening the branch, was held at the Keighley Temperance Hall, attended by the late Bob Cryer MP, and others.

After almost six years of negotiations and hard work by volunteer members, the society ran its official inspection train from Keighley to Oxenhope on the 8th June, 1968, hauled by USA Tank No. 72. This was later followed, on the 29th June, by the re-opening special, double-headed by No. 72 (in American livery of golden brown and silver smoke box) with Ivatt No. 41241 (in maroon livery).

At its main line connection in Keighley, the KWVR uses platforms three and four. Platform four was extended in 1970. Shortly after leaving Keighley, the disused Great Northern line to Queensbury diverged off to the left, which was one of the most heavily engineered lines in Yorkshire, with magnificent viaducts at Hewenden and Thornton and numerous tunnels and cuttings.

The first station met on the KWVR is Ingroe West, originally only a halt, and is now home to the Bahamas Locomotive Society and the Vintage Carriages Trust. The station building was originally situated at Foulridge on the Skipton/Colne line, where it was dismantled, stone by stone, and transferred to Ingroe.

The next station is the tiny Damins Halt and level crossing, quickly followed by Oakworth, of *The Railway Children* fame. The lines' headquarters and locomotive shed is situated at Howarth, where a fine viewing and picnic area, overlooking the yard, has been constructed. The line finally terminates at Oxenhope, which is home to the carriage shed and museum, giving the line a total length of 5 miles.

Howarth

The early nineteenth century inhabitants of the village of Howarth would never have envisaged their village and surroundings to be the famous tourist attraction it is today. The appointment of a vicar and the construction of a branch line railway would, in later years, turn the area into a magnet for visitors.

The Reverend Patrick Brontë and family came from Thornton, near Bradford, to take up the curacy at Howarth. Sadly, his wife Maria and the two eldest daughters, Maria and Elizabeth, all died within five years of their arrival, leaving his only son, Branwell, and three remaining daughters, Charlotte, Emily and Anne. The three sisters took up positions as governesses in various parts of the country, but without any great success and, in due course, all returned to Howarth where they began their writng careers. Branwell, after intervals as an artist and railway clerk, had meanwhile taken to alcohol. In failing health, he spent his last years in the local hostelry, his demise coming in 1848, soon to be followed by Emily and Anne and, later, Charlotte in 1856. The reverend, Patrick, outlived all of his six children, reaching the age of eighty-four.

Howarth today is a village of two halves, divided by Bridgehouse Beck and the railway, the east side more steeply graded, with its rows of four-storey terraced dwellings, the youth hostel, a sandstone quarry and a wind turbine. The west side is dominated by the old parsonage and church, the cobbled main street, with an array of gift shops selling Brontë memorabilia, pubs and cafes, and beyond all of this, the brooding Brontë moorland.

Stage 11 Oakworth station – Newsholme – Goose-Eye

Start	Oakworth station GR 039384
Distance	2.5 miles (4 km) linear 5 miles (8 km) circular
Map	OS Explorer OL21
Parking	(roadside) Station Road

From the station entrance, turn right to ascend Station Road. In 250 metres, turn left to pass through a metalled kissing gate. Cross the pasture with a fence/hedge to the left. After a second gate, advance in the same direction, but now on a tightly enclosed path. The KWVR will now be seen down to the left as it crosses the River Worth. Continue along until nearing a tall stone chimney, and then turn right into a further enclosed way that leads up towards the chimney. Pass a cottage on the left and onto its access drive, which is followed to pass round the chimney and the site of Providence Mill, to gain the Howarth/Oakworth road. Cross and enter the access track opposite, pass Lodge Farm and then beneath a transmission line to arrive at Lower Laithe Barn. Turn right, to follow the footpath sign that directs you to the right of the house and across the lawn, to find the stile in the top right hand corner, which then sends you up the pasture with a wall on the right. On reaching the cross-wall, ignore the gap-stile, but turn left to follow the wall to where it turns right at a gate. Pass through, now in a briefly enclosed tractor track, which admits onto Tim Lane, via a second gate. Turn right here to rise up Tim Lane, and as the grade eases, turn to admire the view back over the Worth valley and Mytholmes, with the outskirts of Howarth beyond. At the road junction, turn left up Denby Hill Road and, in 150 metres, turn right at the bridleway sign. Proceed along the enclosed way (somewhat wet at the time of writing) to a junction where a right turn is made into a further bridleway, where conditions underfoot improve considerably.

After 250 metres, watch for a stone step-stile on the left which sends a good path along a brief terrace to enter woodland. Follow the obvious

Bobbin Mill

route beneath the trees to the exit stile and then out into pasture, with a cemetery up on the right, and grass-covered old quarry workings to the left. Descend to the stile giving access onto Slack Lane. Take Gill Lane opposite, which first drops down to cross Newsholme Beck at the charmingly renovated Old Bobbin Mill and then rises to enter the quaint hamlet of Newsholme. On passing St. Johns Church, the lane bends right, ceases to be surfaced and then divides. Follow the enclosed bridleway going left for 100 metres. Now continue in the same direction along the path, which leads to a stile on the edge of Newsholme Dean. Descend steeply into Cat Clough, eventually arriving at a gate which sends the Way across a pasture to the clapper and tractor bridges spanning Dean Beck.

Continue ahead to two gates and take the one on the right that sends the enclosed track through the idyllically sited Newsholme Dean. Pass to the rear of the final building, Rose Cottage, to find a narrow path, descending right, which comes alongside a crumbling wall and gradually drops down towards the beck. Disregard the footbridge and continue with the beck and mill pond on the right. Cross the beck and then up onto the lane to turn left. (Just before the road turns, to recross the beck, note the

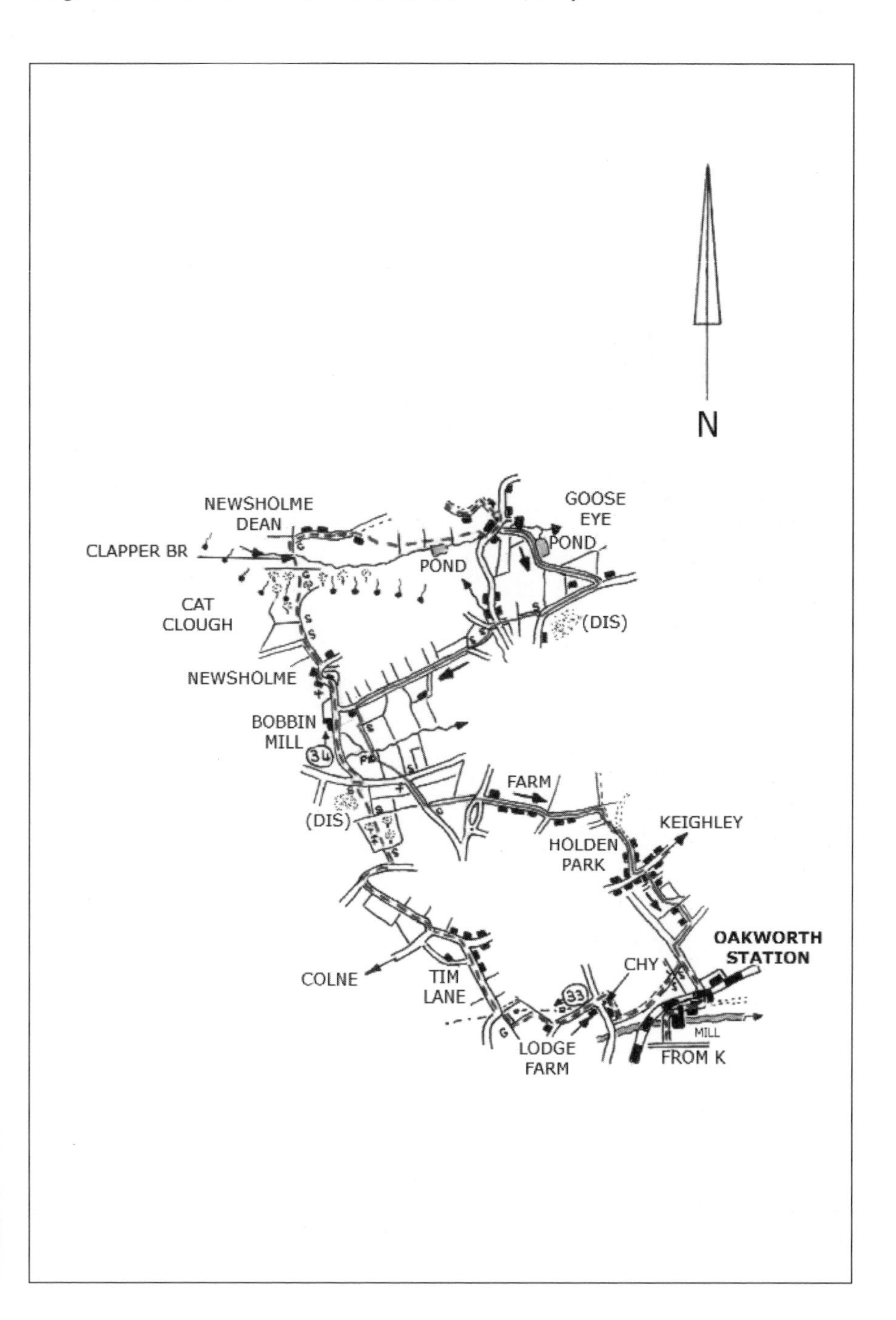
N
NEWSHOLME
DEAN
GOOSE
EYE
CLAPPER BR
POND
POND
CAT
CLOUGH
(DIS)
NEWSHOLME
BOBBIN
MILL
34
FARM
(DIS)
KEIGHLEY
HOLDEN
PARK
OAKWORTH
STATION
CHY
COLNE
TIM
LANE
33
MILL
LODGE
FARM
FROM K

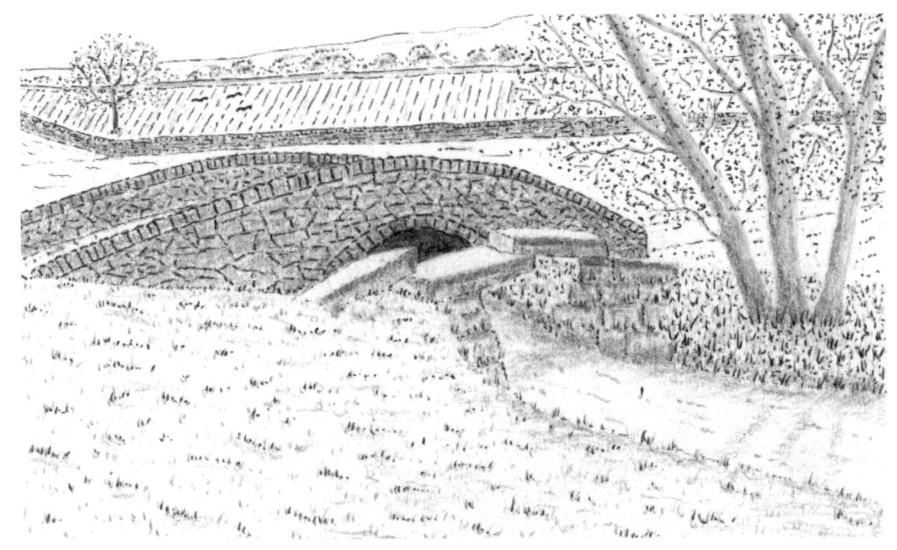

Bridges at Newsholme Dean

cobbled by-way on the right, which is the start of the return route.) Continue ahead to arrive at the Turkey Inn at Goose Eye.

Return Route

Goose Eye to Oakworth Station

From the Turkey Inn, retrace your steps to cross Dean Beck turning immediately left into the cobbled by-way. Pass the converted mill and its pond on the left. Rise up to meet Holme House Lane, where a turn to the right is made. After 250 metres, descend a short bank to locate a gap-stile on the right that sends a slightly discernable path across the pasture with the vestiges of a wall on the right. Pass through a stile/gate in a cross-wall and then advance with an accompanying wall on the left, to gain the lane at Holme House. Cross into the access drive opposite. Immediately after crossing the beck, squeeze through the stile on the left and then rise up the pasture with a wall in tandem on your left. The path enters a short-lived, enclosed way, which admits to a bridleway. Turn right and follow this, passing Higher Laithe on the left where the route becomes surfaced.

On approaching the next cottage, turn left down its gable into an enclosed brief track and, at its end, find a step-stile on the right. Now go left to follow the wall down to the footbridge over Newsholme Beck.

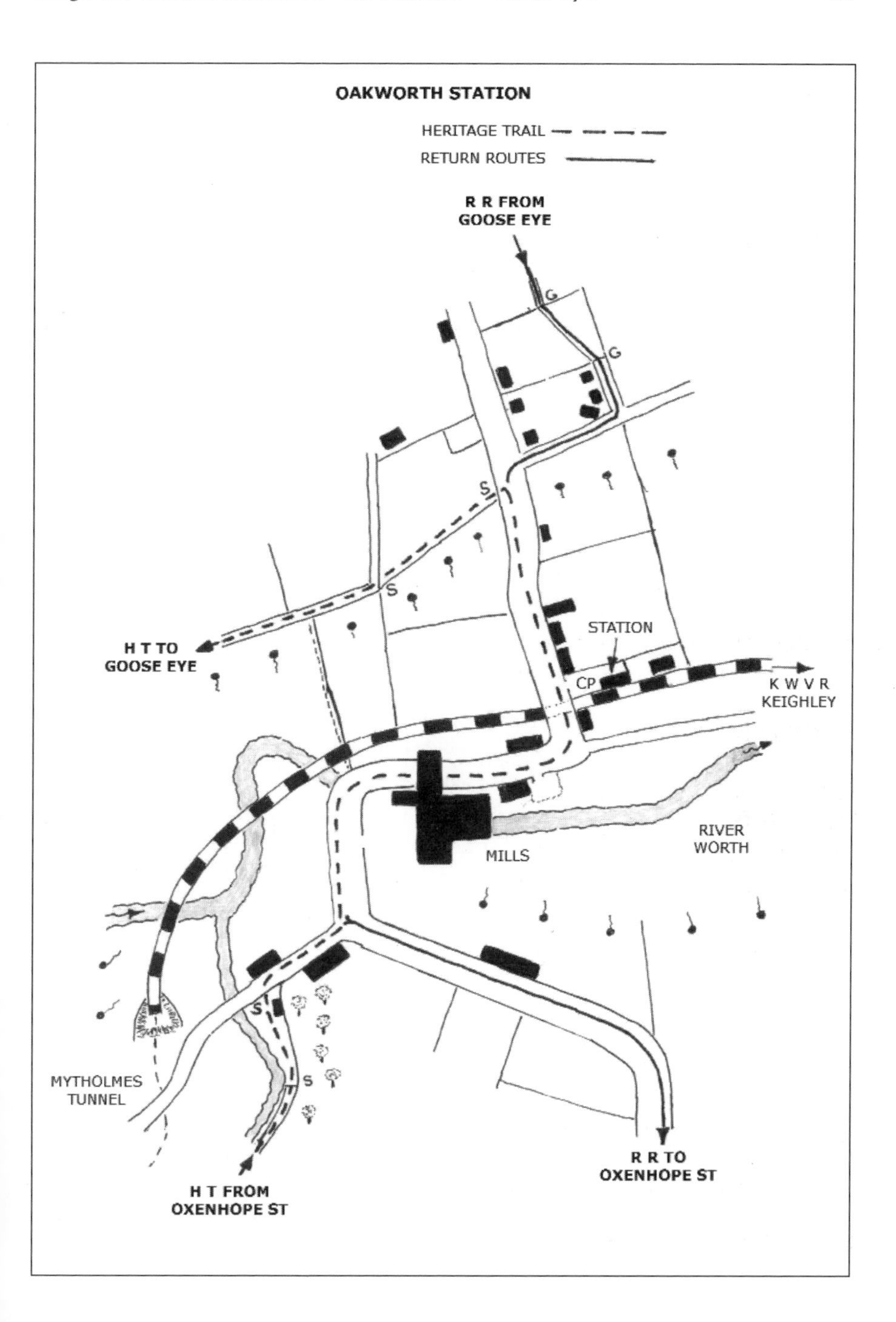
OAKWORTH STATION
HERITAGE TRAIL
RETURN ROUTES
R R FROM GOOSE EYE
G
G
S
S
H T TO GOOSE EYE
STATION
CP
K W V R KEIGHLEY
RIVER WORTH
MILLS
S
S
MYTHOLMES TUNNEL
R R TO OXENHOPE ST
H T FROM OXENHOPE ST

Goose Eye

Following the obvious path up to Slack Lane, go directly across into Wide Lane, with the cemetery on the right. Pass by the memorial gate at Oakworth cricket club and, in 30 metres, advance through a gap on the left leading into a small sports field. Follow the left hand wall that leads down to a gate. Cross over the one way lanes system into the by-way to the right of the farm opposite. Now with the environs of Oakworth on the right, follow the by-way to a junction, turn left and advance into a narrow leafy lane. When this turns sharply right, a gap will be seen ahead in the boundary wall to Holden Park. Pass through and turn left to descend a flight of steps. Follow the wall for 100 metres to a further gap leading into a stony track. Turn right soon gaining the cottages on Clough Lane, which is followed down to its junction with the B6143 at Oakworth. Turn left and rise to the second opening on the right (Lark Street), which is followed down to Larkfield House, after which the route becomes tightly enclosed until a gate admits to a small pasture. Cross to the gate on the left of High East Royd. Advance down its access drive, turning right to admit onto Station Road. Turn left and descend 400 metres to regain Oakworth station.

Stage 12: Goose Eye to Sutton-in-Craven (Kings Arms)

Start	Turkey Inn – Goose Eye GR 028406
Distance	2.5 miles (4 km) linear 6 miles (9.5 km) circular
Map	OS Explorer OL21
Parking	Roadside/pub (with permission)

With your back to the Turkey Inn, turn left along the road and, in 50 metres, take the unsurfaced lane on the left. Pass the cottages on the right and then turn sharp left at the footpath signs. At the entrance gate to Bow End, turn right to enter an enclosed path passing to the rear of the house. On reaching a wider track, turn sharp right up towards Clough Bank and its adjacent transmission pylon. Turn left up the access drive which soon leads onto Todley Hall Lane. Turn left to rise up the lane, first passing Todley Hall and then Dob Field Farm, both of which are on the left with Newsholme hamlet and Cat Clough in view beyond. Approximately 200 metres after passing Dob Field, watch carefully for a step-stile on the right. Cross and rise up the pasture with a wall in tandem on the left. The path now follows the wall unerringly over Todley Hill, passing over seven stiled cross-walls to eventually gain the lane at Pole Stoop, where a left turn is made.

As you walk along the lane, the top of Lunds Tower on Earl Crag will be seen ahead. Half-left in the far distance, Top Withins on the Pennine Way may also be visible. Continue along the lane and, shortly before reaching High Pole Farm, turn right into the unsurfaced America Lane. Advance along the enclosed track, now with views of Sutton and Airedale ahead. Soon a footpath sign will be met, which directs you left through a gate down to America Farm. Follow the well signed route, passing between the immaculately maintained properties and down the wooden steps into the pasture. Descend the field with the wall to your left. Pass through a gate and aim half-left to join the access drive to the farm ahead. Enter the yard, immediately turning right to advance through a gate. Turn right

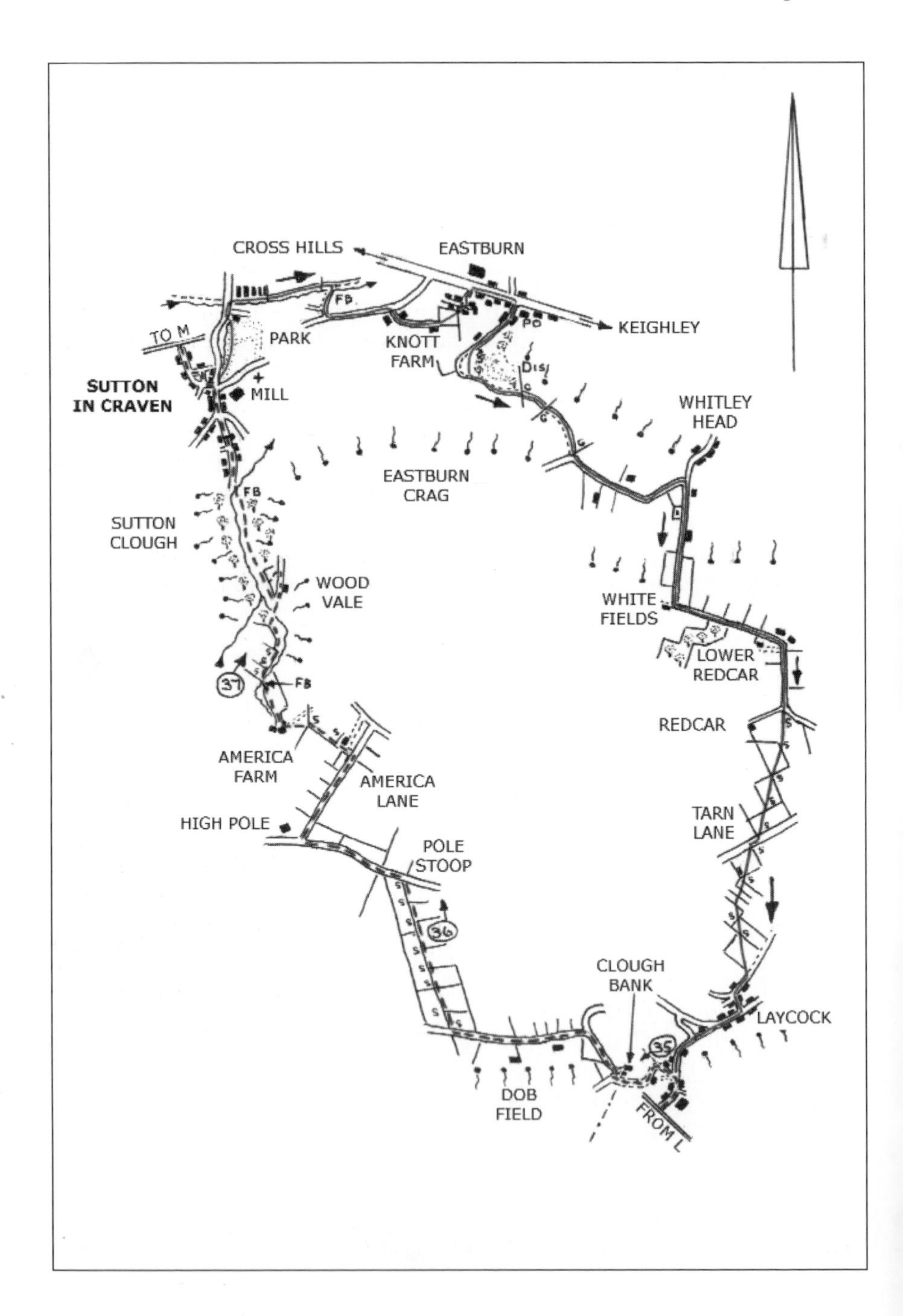
CROSS HILLS
EASTBURN
KEIGHLEY
FB
TO M
PARK
KNOTT
FARM
PO
DIS
SUTTON
IN CRAVEN
MILL
WHITLEY
HEAD
EASTBURN
CRAG
FB
SUTTON
CLOUGH
WOOD
VALE
WHITE
FIELDS
LOWER
REDCAR
37
FB
REDCAR
AMERICA
FARM
AMERICA
LANE
TARN
LANE
HIGH POLE
POLE
STOOP
36
CLOUGH
BANK
LAYCOCK
35
DOB
FIELD
FROM L

again, now on a path between a wall with a beck to the right. As the route admits into pasture the beck disappears underground, soon to reappear over the wall on the left. Follow the wall carefully, as it descends into the clough, to find a well hidden stone slab footbridge. Rise up the opposite bank, turning right and follow the boundary fence. After negotiating two cross-stiles, cross a third, after which the fence should be on your **left**, now on a fine path with the beck down to the right and beneath a canopy of leaves. Soon the path becomes enclosed between the vestiges of walls and zig-zags down to a bridge. (10 metres beyond the bridge, you can turn left at the remnants of a stile to follow the beck downstream. Though this is not a right of way, thousands of boots have passed this way.) The official way is to continue ahead, rising up the boggy track to pass through Wood Vale Farm and out via its access drive. In 100 metres, go over the stile on the left, then diagonally left down the field and over the stile to rejoin the beckside path. There now follows a grand easy stride down Lumb Clough, always on the beck's right bank. Eventually, pass over a fine wooden bridge and proceed down Hall Drive to pass out beneath the impressive arched entrance lodge, which was the gateway to the now demolished Sutton Hall.

Sutton Hall Gateway

Advance to the junction and continue down Sutton's High Street to arrive at the Kings Arms, on the corner with North Street.

Return Route

Sutton – Eastburn – Laycock – Goose-Eye

From the Kings Arms, continue ahead passing the public toilets and the Black Bull and then, to avoid road walking, enter Sutton Park. Follow the beck through the gardens and at their end, regain the roadway. Immediately after crossing Holme Beck, take the signed path on the right. This sends the Way between housing and the beck. Pass through a kissing gate into an enclosed path that parallels the beck. On reaching a footbridge, cross and then follow the road to Sutton Lane and then turn left (beware – no footway). In 400 metres, turn right into Knott Lane. Rise up, passing the cattery and kennels and then along the front of the converted Knott Farm to find a gap-stile and steps leading into a rough pasture. Descend diagonally to a small gate, giving access to a short-lived, enclosed path. At its end, turn right up the avenue and in 20 metres, take the signed path on the left, which passes between housing and then to the right of a colony of garages, to emerge onto the main road at Eastburn. Turn right up the now quiet road, passing the Eastburn Inn. On reaching the post office, turn right into Moor Lane, which is paved with two tracks of stone pavings, indicating its former use as a quarry access road.

After passing through housing, the lane turns right and enters woodland, at which point it steepens considerably. On emerging from beneath the trees, take the narrower path rising up on the left, with strategically placed seating to appreciate the view looking back over Airedale. The path comes alongside a stone wall to rejoin the original wider track, which has taken a more circuitous route. Continue to rise on the obvious way that turns left as the climb eases. On the left is the massive disused Eastburn quarry, now screened by trees. After passing through a gate, the track becomes an enclosed green way, which is now followed unfailingly as it rises up to a junction. Turn left onto the surfaced intake lane, with fine views across Airedale to Silsden, with the western end of Rombalds Moor beyond. (There now follows one mile of road walking, thankfully on quiet lanes, Seeton moor suffering from a dirth of footpaths.)

Pass Brigton Farm and descend to the junction at Whitley Head. Turn right onto Redcar Lane that rises steeply, again with convenient seating. The climb levels and the lane turns sharp left at White Fields Farm, then

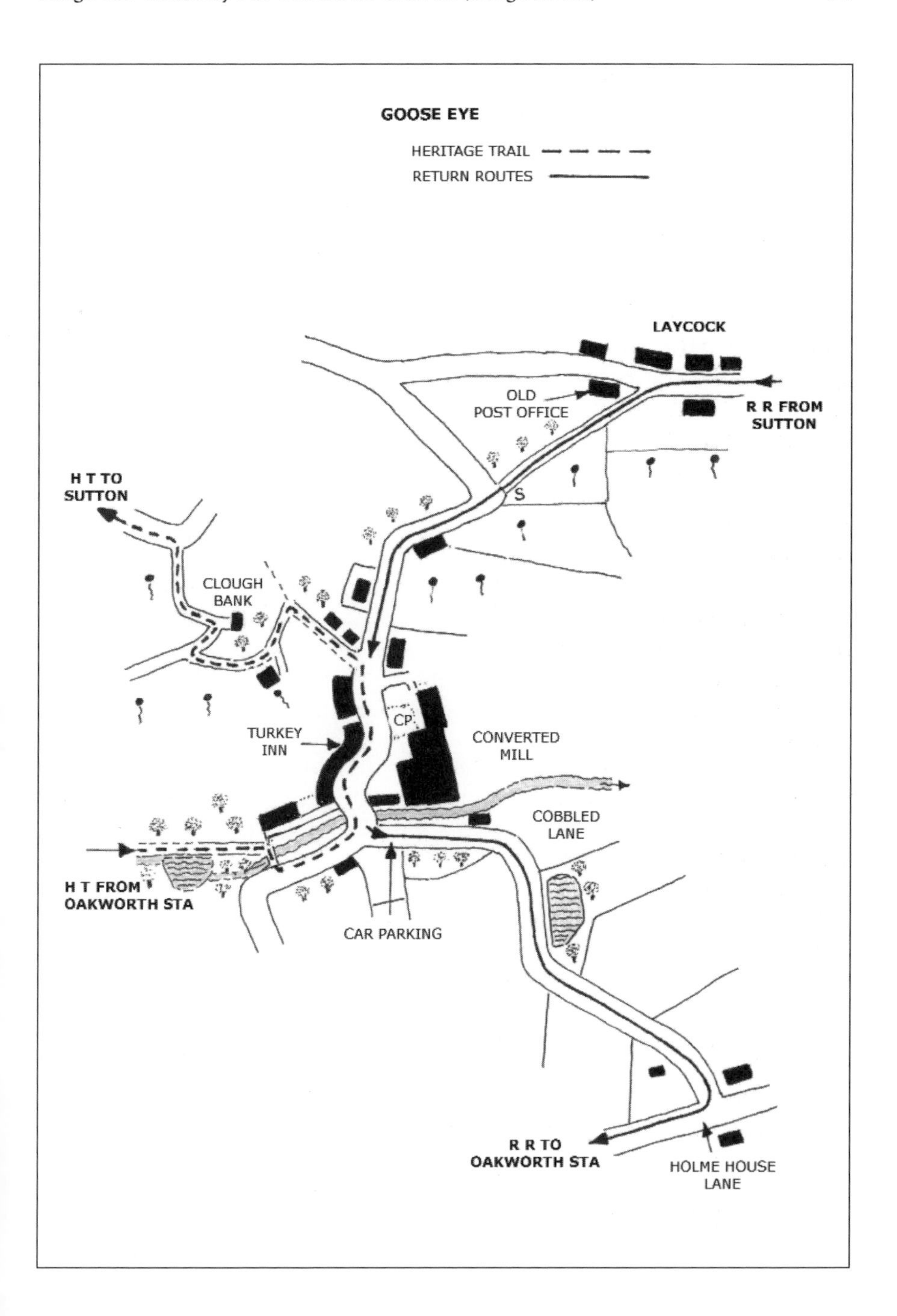
GOOSE EYE
HERITAGE TRAIL
RETURN ROUTES
LAYCOCK
OLD POST OFFICE
R R FROM SUTTON
H T TO SUTTON
S
CLOUGH BANK
CP
TURKEY INN
CONVERTED MILL
COBBLED LANE
H T FROM OAKWORTH STA
CAR PARKING
R R TO OAKWORTH STA
HOLME HOUSE LANE

right at Lower Redcar, now renovated into two separate dwellings. The lane now rises slightly and turns left, at which point take the signed path ahead, which directs you across the field to a stile 75 metres to the left of the prominent gate. Cross the next meadow to a stile in the top corner. The Way now follows obvious stiles to eventually emerge onto Tarn Lane. Turn right and, in 50 metres, follow the signed path on the left to pass through a smallholding, after which follow the numerous stiles unerringly down to enter a walled green lane. Follow this, passing cottages to the junction with a surfaced road. Turn left and descend to the main street at Laycock. Turn right to walk through the charming village and, on reaching the old post office, delve to the left on the signed path which becomes tightly enclosed with causey stones underfoot. At its end, continue ahead onto the lane that descends steeply down to Goose Eye and the Turkey Inn.

Laycock

Sutton-in-Craven

Like other northern villages, Sutton-in-Craven owes its existence to its situation on water courses, in this case the becks of Lumb and Holme. Originally, spinning and weaving took place in farms and cottages, giving us the saying 'home spun yarn'. Soon, entrepreneurs had small weaving shops erected where they could employ staff, thus eliminating the need for 'letting out'. As the textile revolution grew, larger premises were required. Greenroyd spinning mill was founded by the first Peter Hartley in the early 19th century and the business was passed on to his eldest son John. On his demise in 1848, his youngest brother William inherited to continue the business until 1883, and was then inherited by his only son, John William Hartley. William Jnr. lived at Sutton Hall, built in 1894 on the west bank of Lumb Clough. The impressive entrance archway on Hall Drive, containing the Hartley trade mark, still stands today, the hall itself now demolished.

Greenroyd Mill was sold in 1911 to James Bairstow and was used for worsted spinning and manufacture during the next five years. Greenroyd continued in the ownership of T. and M. Bairstow until 1966 when it was sold to W. Hutchinson (Yarns) Ltd. of Bradford. Production followed until 1980, but with the decline in the textile industry, sadly, Greenroyd Mill closed its doors, after 150 years in operation, making all its employees redundant., ending an era. Today,

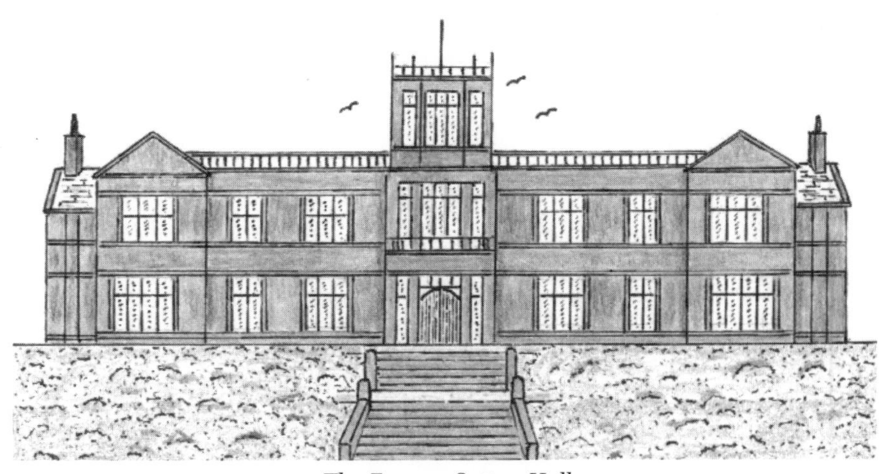

The Former Sutton Hall

Greenroyd Mill still stands empty, but with plans to convert the buildings into apartments. Sutton Mill also closed with the loss of hundreds of jobs. The buildings were demolished in 1996.

Present day Sutton has become a pleasant residential village with people commuting to neighbouring towns for employment and shopping.

Stage 13: Sutton-in-Craven (Kings Arms) to Silsden (Bridge End Inn)

Start	**Village centre GR 006441**
Distance	**4 miles (6.5 km) linear** **7 miles (11.3 km) circular**
Map	**OS Explorer OL21**
Parking	**High Street**

From the Kings Arms, turn into North Road. In 15 metres, advance down the unsurfaced way ahead and pass beneath the archway at Gibraltar Terrace to turn left along the short-lived Elm Road, at the end of which turn right and, at the next junction, continue ahead along Hazel Grove. This leads into an enclosed path that descends to a footbridge over Holme Beck. Continue ahead passing cottages on the left and then into an enclosed path (Shutt Lane), which merges onto the A6068 Colne road at Glusburn. Go directly across to squeeze between cottages into an unpaved way, with farmyard/scrapyard on the right. Pass through a gap-stile on the right that sends a tightly enclosed footway rising between housing, and, at its end, cross the estate road to enter a walled lane which leads up past a charmingly restored farmhouse. On arriving at a gate, pass through and turn sharp right.

Continue ahead between Ryecroft Farm and barn. The path now becomes briefly enclosed before entering pastureland. Follow the obvious way, which shortly turns right and then angles left, passing between housing to emerge onto Park Road. Now turn right and descend to the junction. Continue ahead for 150 metres until attaining Lindley House on the left, immediately after which, turn left to find a gate and stile. Advance down, turning first right then, shortly, leave the track taking the faint path left, descending to a kissing gate. Proceed along the enclosed way that admits onto Station Road. Turn left to pass over the Keighley/Skipton rail line and, in 200 metres, on approaching the junction with the A629 trunk road, take the paved pathway on the left, which passes beneath the roadway and emerges onto the old A629.

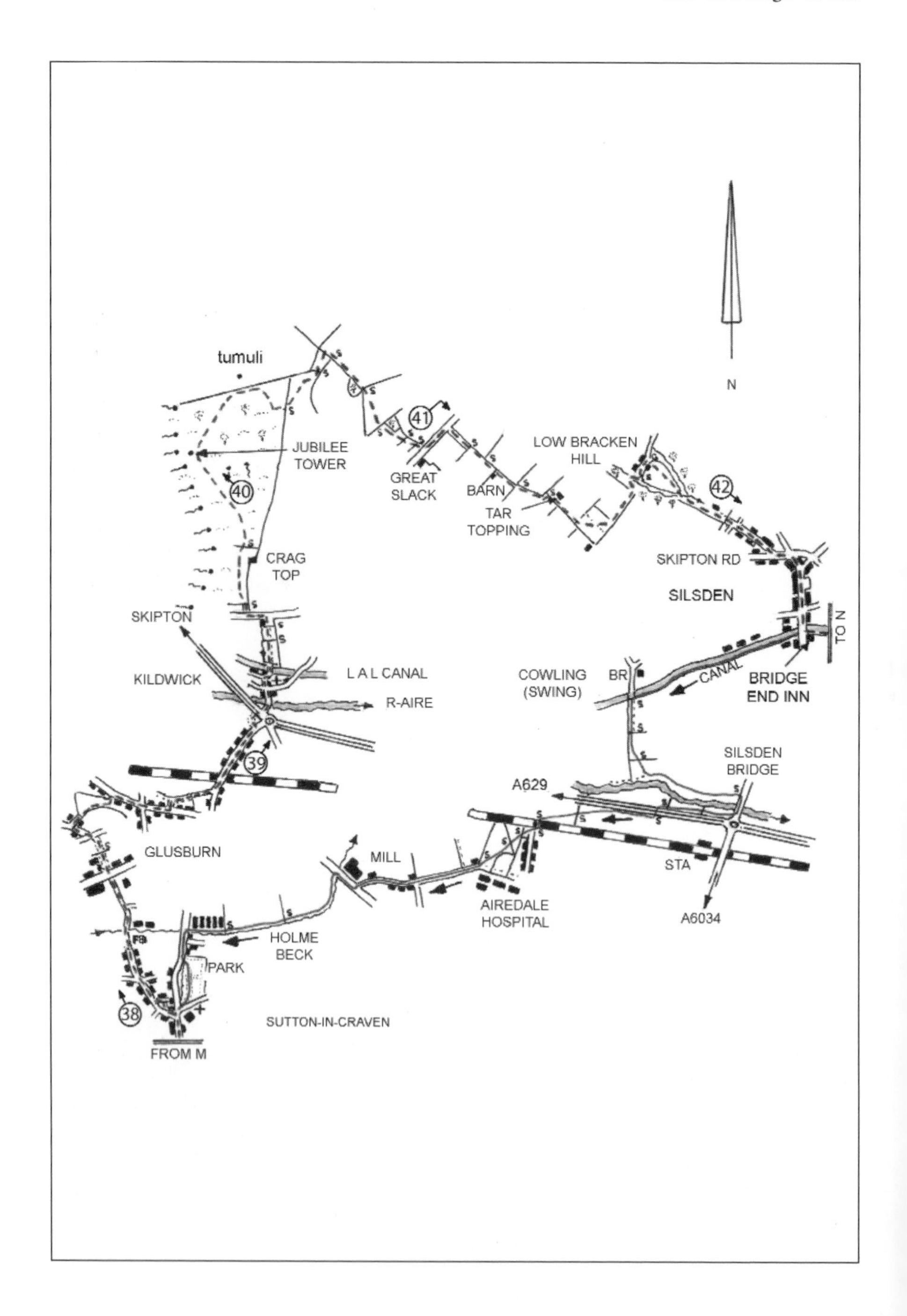
N
tumuli
JUBILEE
TOWER
40
41
GREAT
SLACK
BARN
TAR
TOPPING
LOW BRACKEN
HILL
42
SKIPTON RD
SILSDEN
TO N
CRAG
TOP
SKIPTON
KILDWICK
L A L CANAL
R-AIRE
39
COWLING
(SWING)
BR
CANAL
BRIDGE
END INN
SILSDEN
BRIDGE
A629
GLUSBURN
MILL
STA
AIREDALE
HOSPITAL
A6034
HOLME
BECK
FB
PARK
38
SUTTON-IN-CRAVEN
FROM M

Cross the bridge over the River Aire and rise up to the junction at Kildwick village (note the milestone on the left).

From the village centre, take the road going uphill with St. Andrews church to the right. Turn first right at Kirkgate and then left round the corner of the old schoolhouse (dated 1839). Now ascend up to the footbridge crossing the Leeds/Liverpool canal. This is a delectable spot with the church, the old schoolhouse, and a paved way up to the stone footbridge. Continue ahead, rising on a fine flagged path under a ceiling of foliage and a stream to the left. Pass through two small gateways to gain the entrance drive to the old vicarage.

On reaching the lane, turn left to descend into a dip, soon to meet Stonegate Cottage on the left. Directly across, a footpath sign sends a path through a gate on its way to Farnhill Moor. Follow the obvious way to a gate on the left of Crag Top Farm. The route now rises unfailingly through heather and bracken to suddenly find itself at the Jubilee monument, built to commemorate the silver jubilee of King George V in 1935, which is depicted on a nearby rockface. The view over Airedale from the monument is wonderful. Starting in the south-west is Earl Crag

Jubilee Tower

and its two towers, beyond which the tip of Lad Law is visible. Across the dale is the chimney of the old smelting mill on Gib Side, with Cononley below. To the north, Sharp Haw, Rough Haw and Crook Rise Crag are all on show.

From the monument, take the path going north, still with heather, bracken and, now also, silver birch trees. Eventually a stone wall and seat will be met. On the far side of the wall is the site of a tummuli (burial ground) and long cairn. Proceed with the wall on the left for 250 metres and then angle right for 100 metres, then go left on a narrower path to soon arrive at a step-stile. Now in pastureland, follow the distinct path left to a step-stile in the field corner. Angle slightly away from the right hand boundary to a second stile in the cross-wall, turning immediately right. Now follow the well signed path over five stiles to eventually arrive at Great Slack on New Lane. Turn left along the lane for 100 metres and then turn right into a briefly enclosed green lane. Pass over a step-stile and continue ahead with an accompanying wall to the left. Follow the wall, first passing to the left of a small barn, then angling round to the left to arrive at the stile and gate at the ruined Tar Topping.

Tar Topping

Cross the stile and turn right, with the ruins to your left. The route now delves into a short lived, leafy, enclosed way and then through two gateless gaps, after which angle 45° left to the far corner of the field.

Ignoring the stile on the right, advance through the gap ahead with a boundary on the right towards the woodland seen ahead.

On reaching the trees, the path joins a paved tractor track that descends to a charming corner where it crosses the beck via a stone bridge. The Way then rises, turning left to gain the gate into the yard at Low Bracken Hill Farm. Pass through the yard to find the small gate to the left of the farmhouse. Follow the waymarker which sends the path down the left hand boundary of a large, narrowing pasture. Locate the gate and rough steps at its end, then ford the beck, which is followed downstream. Soon the right of way emerges into a smallholding and plant depot. Pass through the gap to the right of the entrance gates. Now in the environs of Silsden, continue ahead down the unmade road that leads into Foster Avenue. At the junction, turn left into Skipton Road and then right into Briggate. Now turn right down Kirkgate, which is crossed by the pelican. Continue ahead to the canal bridge and steps by the side of the Bridge End pub.

Return Route

Silsden to Sutton

Continue down the steps to the left of the Bridge End pub onto the towpath of the Leeds/Liverpool canal and turn left to pass beneath the road bridge. On the right now are the workshops and hire base of Silsden Boats. Continue along, noting the enviably sited houses, some of which have their own private moorings. On reaching the first swing bridge (Cowling Bridge), leave the towpath by taking the stile on the left. Now follow the obvious waymarked path over stiles down to the River Aire. Turn **left** now with the river on your right again, follow the distinct path to the stile leading onto the road at Silsden Bridge. Turn right to cross the River Aire via Silsden Bridge. In 50 metres, cross the stile on the right, which sends the route across a small pasture to a stone slab footbrige over a sidestream. Now follow the riverside path under a canopy of leaves. When a stone wall and step-stile are met, cross and leave the riverside. Angle left to a stile and sign leading up to the A629 trunk road and cross with care to find the stile on the opposite side.

Turn right, keeping to the boundary fence and continue ahead into the next field to a footpath sign in the boundary fence. This directs you to angle half-left away from the fence to a step-stile in a cross-wall. Continue in the same direction to the level crossing over the Keighley/Skipton

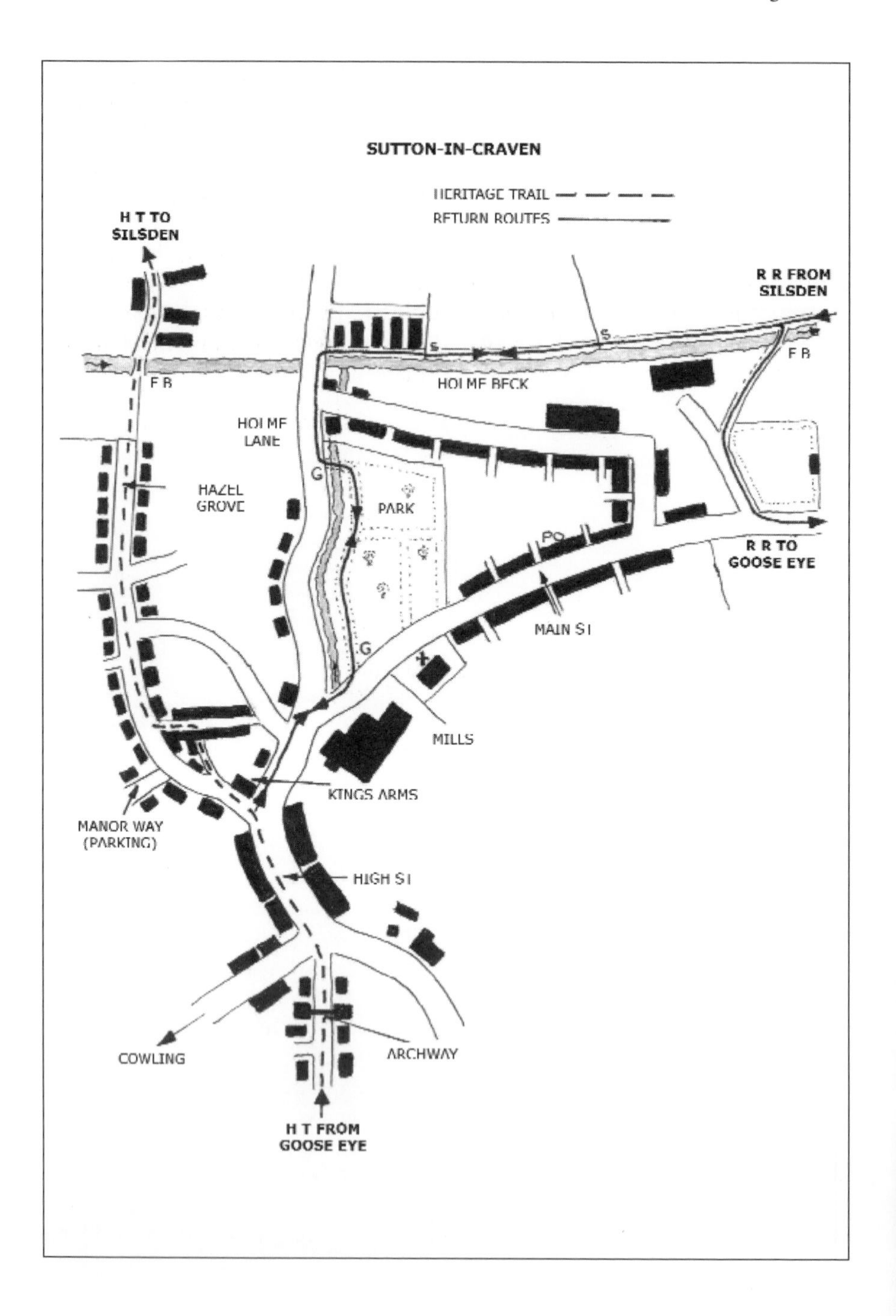
SUTTON-IN-CRAVEN
HERITAGE TRAIL
RETURN ROUTES
H T TO
SILSDEN
R R FROM
SILSDEN
S
S
F B
F B
HOLME BECK
HOLME
LANE
HAZEL
GROVE
G
PARK
G
PO
R R TO
GOOSE EYE
MAIN ST
MILLS
KINGS ARMS
MANOR WAY
(PARKING)
HIGH ST
COWLING
ARCHWAY
H T FROM
GOOSE EYE

railway. Again, cross with care, turn right and over a stile into pastureland. After passing over a second stile, the path comes alongside a wire fence. Follow this to its junction with a farm track where a right turn is made. The buildings on the left are part of Airedale General Hospital. Continue along the track, which soon becomes enclosed and then surfaced, at which point it becomes Lyon Road. Advance along, passing charming cottages on the left and then through Lyon Farm to arrive at the Crosshills/Seaton road, which we cross and turn right. In 100 metres, pass over Holme Beck and immediately go left onto the beckside path which is followed unfailingly to Holme Lane at Sutton. Turn left and avoid road walking by taking the path through Sutton Park to return to the start at the Kings Arms.

Silsden and the Leeds - Liverpool Canal

The name Silsden is derived from two Saxon words – sighle (farmer) and dean (land in a hollow). The village lies to the north of the River Aire and below the western edge of Rombolds Moor. In the doomsday book, it is depicted as the most important village in Craven – even upstaging Skipton.

King William gave the manor of Silsden to Robert de Romille in 1090. In 1185, the order of Knights Templars owned land in Silsden, until subdued in 1322 when their land was held by the order of St. John of Jerusalem.

In the mid 18th century, over two hundred smithies who manufactured nails resided in Silsden and surrounding areas. The trade was to last for almost a century, until mechanised methods took over.

In 1778 the Leeds/Liverpool canal arrived in Silsden, where a wharf and warehouse were constructed for the loading and unloading of merchandise. The canal was the most successful and longest canal in Britain. One of the main reasons for this was its sheer size at 127 miles in length. Also, the area through which it passes was heavily populated and was the heart of the textile manufacturing revolution. The first survey of the original route between Leeds and Preston, with branches to Lancaster and Liverpool, was undertaken by John Longbottom in 1765.

Eventually, after much disagreement and manoeuvring, an act was passed in parliament for the building of the canal from Leeds to Liverpool via Bingley, Shipley, Keighley, Silsden, Skipton, Burnley, Blackburn and Wigan. Construction began in 1770 from both ends simultaneously. The Yorkshire side, from Leeds to Gargrave, was completed fairly quickly. However, on the Lancashire side, work was completed as far as the junction with the Douglas Navigation, but then finance evaporated. The two sections over the Pennines were finally connected much later in 1816. The commercial life of the canal ceased in or around the 1950s. Now, of course, like the majority of other canals, their potential for leisure has been realised. Indeed, Silsden has its own longboat hire centre off Elliott Street.

Stage 14: Silsden to Addingham

Start	Bridge End Inn GR 042462
Distance	5 miles (8 km) linear 9 miles (14.5 km) circular
Map	OS Explorer OL21
Parking	Elliot Street (roadside)

Descend the steps to the side of the Bridge Inn and gain the towpath of the Leeds/Liverpool canal. With the water to your left, enjoy the idyllically situated properties on the opposite bank, most of which have their own private moorings. On reaching the first bridge (Brunthwaite swing bridge), cross and leave the canal to rise up the short lived lane to its junction with Holden Lane. Turn right and, in 50 metres, go over the step-stile on the left, which gives access to an enclosed path with the golf course on the right and Brunthwaite Beck to the left. Pass through a gate and immediately over a stone flagged footbridge. Now follow the beck upstream to a stile leading onto the lane. Turn left and enter the charming hamlet of Brunthwaite.

Follow the wall and beck round to the right of the village green. Ascend the steps on the left that send a signed path up the pasture. Pass over three obvious step-stiles to emerge onto the lane at Swartha. Turn right and, in 50 metres, negotiate the stile on the right. Keep to the right hand boundary over which is Swartha Farm. Pass over a substantial stile into the farm's intake track. Follow this as it delves down to cross a small beck. Now go left over the stile and rise up the pasture towards Higher Swartha Farm. Pass to the right of house via another massive stile. Continue to rise with outbuilding and old tractors down to the left. Angle right to find a stile hidden round a corner in the wall up on the right. Once through, continue ahead with a wall in tandem on the right. Cross a beck and stile, then keep to the right of a solitary tree and then to the left of a small, disused overgrown quarry. Now follow the waymarks up to North End Farm, which can be seen above.

Enter the yard, passing the front of the house, where a waymark sends you up the field with a wall on the right to find a small brown gate in the

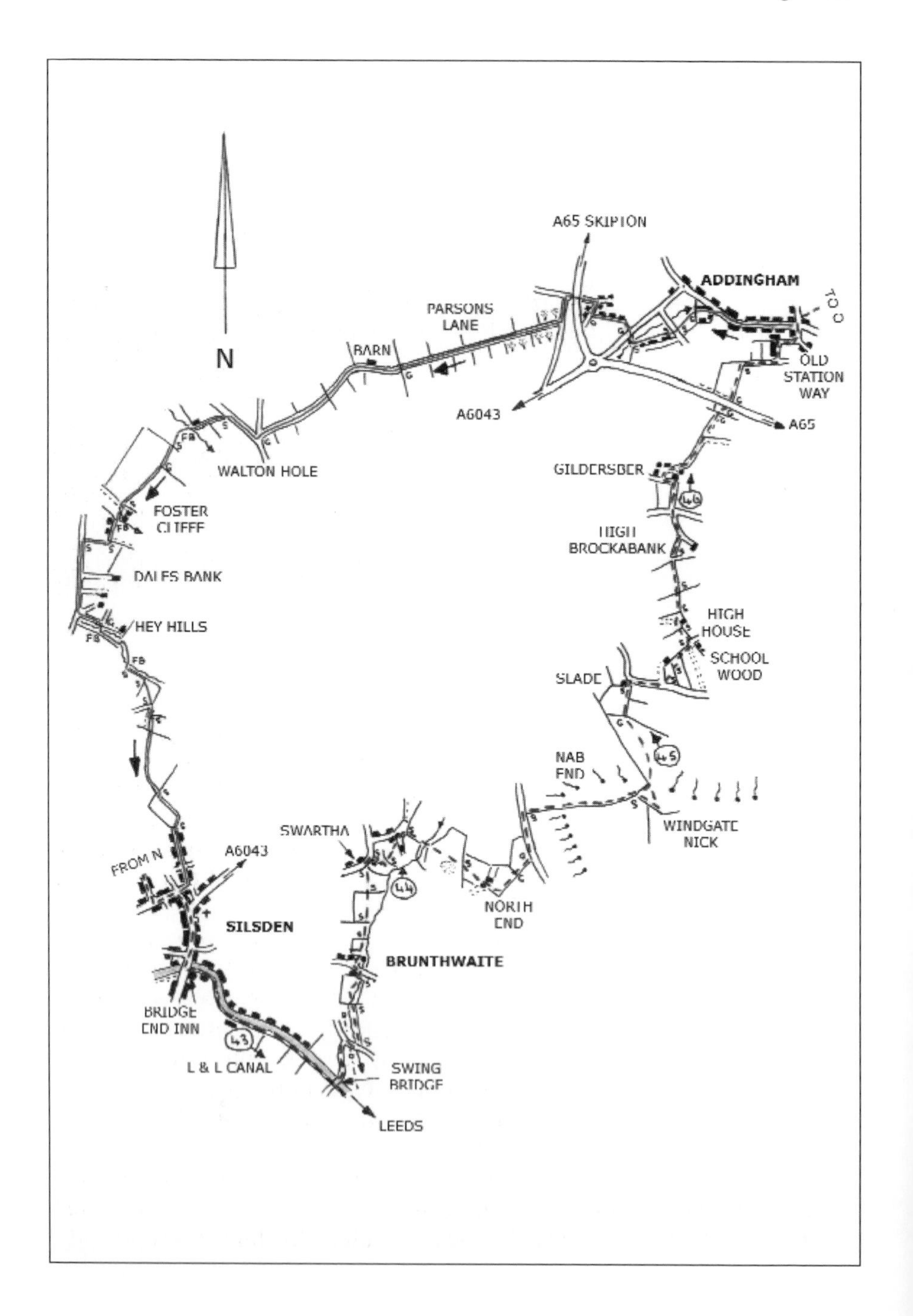
N
A65 SKIPTON
ADDINGHAM
PARSONS LANE
BARN
OLD STATION WAY
A6043
A65
WALTON HOLE
GILDERSBER
46
FOSTER CLIFFE
HIGH BROCKABANK
DALES BANK
HEY HILLS
HIGH HOUSE
SCHOOL WOOD
SLADE
45
NAB END
WINDGATE NICK
SWARTHA
FROM N
A6043
44
NORTH END
SILSDEN
BRUNTHWAITE
BRIDGE END INN
43
L & L CANAL
SWING BRIDGE
LEEDS

North End Farm

corner. Do **not** cross, but turn left and follow the wall passing through two gates to reach Lightbank Lane. Turn left for 200 metres and then over the stile on the right. Now follows a short climb to the summit of Nab End on the western end of Rombolds Moor, where you are rewarded for your efforts by magnificent views over Airedale. (Below is Silsden and the Leeds/Liverpool canal, while across the dale is Steeton and Crosshills, and lower down the valley the town of Keighley, with Brontë moorland beyond.) There now follows a grand stride on a fine green path with White Crag Plantation over the wall on the right. Views down into Wharfedale appear on the left. At the end of the plantation, go right over the stone step-stile. Our way turns left to follow the wall, but a detour up to the seat on the skyline at Windgate Nick (line of ancient route over a ridge) may be made if time allows. Views from here are impressive – across the dale is Beamsley Beacon with Barden Fell and Great Whernside beyond. Below to the right is Addingham and Ilkley.

Retrace your steps down to the stile and wall. Follow the wall that soon turns left, as does the path, distancing itself from the wall as it descends the moor. Soon the intake gate will be met. Follow the faint track down to

Slade Farm at Moorside Lane. Turn right and, 30 metres beyond the entrance to Hodsons Farm, take the signed path on the left, which directs the route across two pastures towards School Wood Farm. Do not enter the yard, but follow the drive going left and then, when the drive turns right, pass over the stile on the left. Now head towards Higher House. Pass to the left of the buildings and round to the rear, then over the step-stile in the corner, with the boundary for company on the right. Advance through two fields to then enter into a tightly enclosed path, which descends to the access drive to High Brockabank. Turn left to pass over a cattle-grid and then continue along to Cocking Lane.

Go directly across and up the drive to Gildersber Farm. Do not enter the farm, but turn left for 10 metres to pass through the gate on the right. Follow the signed path round the rear of the house and pass over a stile into the yard. Continue ahead through two gates out onto the tractor track. Follow this to its end, then over a stile and across a small field to the gate leading onto the A65 trunk road. Cross with care, pass through the gate to continue down the pasture. Turn right to pass over a stile leading into an enclosed path, which soon emerges into the environs of Addingham. Turn left down Southfield Terrace and then right into an enclosed way that soon descends, by steps, into Old Station Way. Turn left to arrive at Main Street.

The Return Route

Addingham (Old Station Way) to Silsden (Bridge End Inn)

Turn left up Main Street for 400 metres, then left into Townhead industrial estate and pass through the small complex to find a gate in the far fence, which gives access to pastureland. Follow Marchup Beck upstream until a walled embankment, carrying an access road, will be seen. Angle left, rising away from the beck to find the stile leading onto the road. Go directly across and follow the obvious path, again with Marchup Beck alongside. Pass through a stile and then cross a side beck via a footbridge. Turn immediate right to cross Marchup Beck via stepping stones. Now rise up the steps, angling right to gain access to an enclosed path with allotments on the left. Cross directly over the A6034 into the playing field and turn left up its right hand boundary to locate the stile onto Turner Lane. Turn right and, in 200 metres, turn left at the dead end sign. Rise up the short lived section of lane and pass through the gate to cross the A65. Once across, ignore the lane directly ahead, but turn left walking parallel to the A65 for 200 metres. Now turn right up the tree-

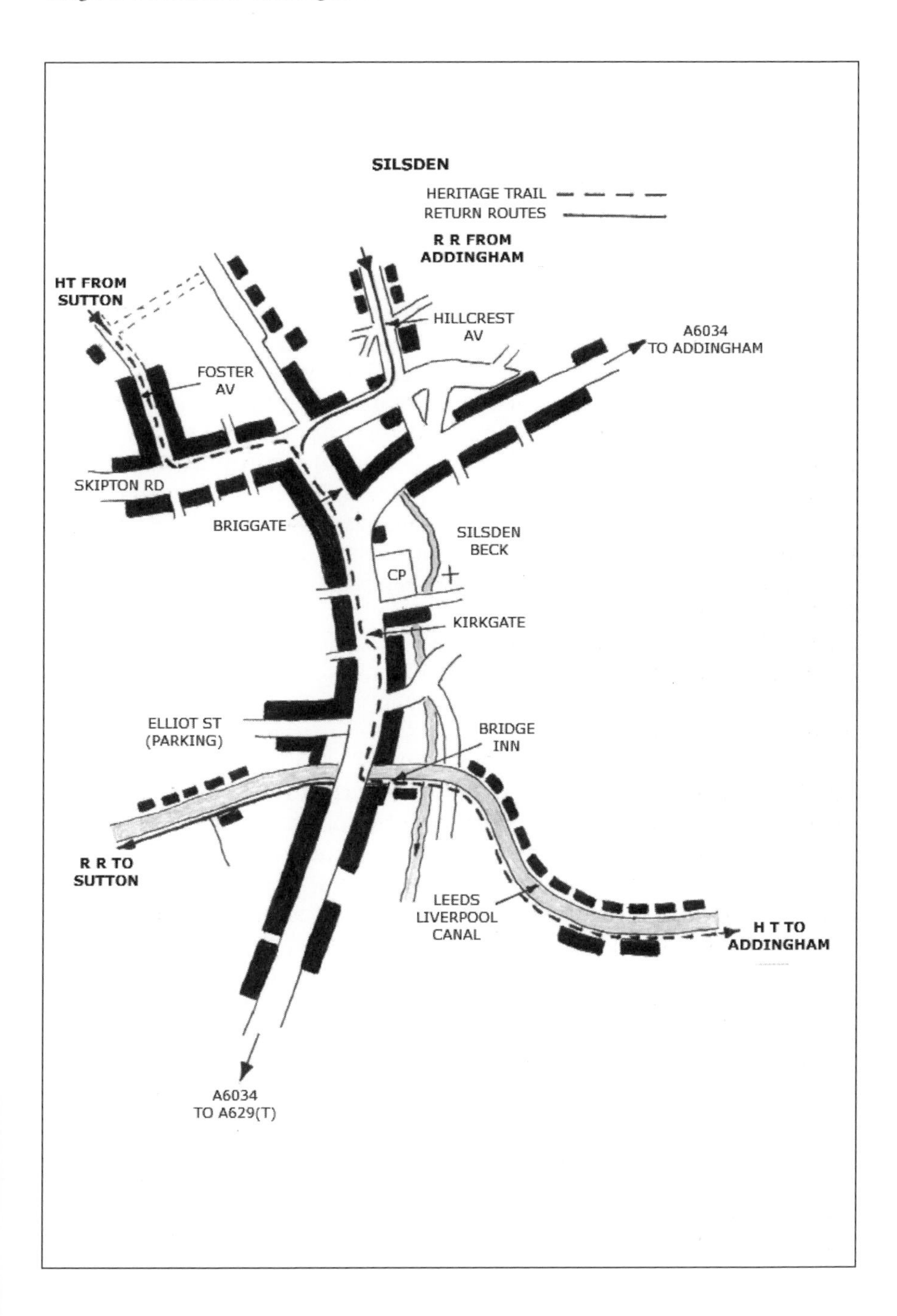
SILSDEN
HERITAGE TRAIL
RETURN ROUTES
R R FROM ADDINGHAM
HT FROM SUTTON
HILLCREST AV
A6034 TO ADDINGHAM
FOSTER AV
SKIPTON RD
BRIGGATE
SILSDEN BECK
CP
KIRKGATE
ELLIOT ST (PARKING)
BRIDGE INN
R R TO SUTTON
LEEDS LIVERPOOL CANAL
H T TO ADDINGHAM
A6034 TO A629(T)

lined Parsons Lane (track), after half a mile of dead straight walking, two gates will be met. Take the one on the left. Parsons Lane now becomes a wide bridleway or drove road (initially, a line of causey stones will be seen on the left hand side). Continue along this ancient route until its end at the gate leading onto Bank Lane.

Turn right onto **Cringles Lane** (not Bank Lane) and, in 200 metres, go left at the footpath sign, which sends you down the access drive to Walton Hole Farm (presently under restoration). Note the engraving above the doorway – HFA 1719. Pass to the front of the buildings and through a gate ahead. Now drop down to cross the footbridge spanning Cowburn Beck. Climb the bank and then angle left to find a raised stony bank. Follow this to a metal gate, now with a fence in tandem on the right, continuing until a stile and gate appear in it. Cross, now with the boundary on the left, continue in the same direction, soon arriving at the access drive to Foster Cliffe House. Go over the metal stile on the left of the electric gate and then turn right to gain the footbridge over Foster Cliffe Beck. Follow the right hand boundary, admiring the array of used tyres and scrap vehicles at the farm as you go! Cross an access drive via two stiles and then turn right to accompany the right hand hedge to attain the stile admitting onto Low Lane. Turn left and descend the quiet lane to pass the entrance to Dales Bank caravan park. Take the next drive on the left (signed B&B at Pickersgill Manor). On reaching the entrance to Ivy House, pass through the gate on the right. Cross over Hey Hills Beck and follow the path down into the pasture below Ivy House. Follow the right hand boundary and beck as they curve right to a stile and slab footbridge in the field corner. Cross and then turn left down the field side. Cross a stile and angle right, aiming for the right hand corner of Hay Hills Farm. Go over the stile into the access lane. Cross the stile opposite that leads into an enclosed track. After 50 metres, go over a delapidated step-stile on the left. Turn immediately right and follow the boundary through two fields to find a stile and small slab-bridge. Enter a brief enclosure that is left by an obvious gap-stile. Turn left to follow the boundary round two sides of the field and then out via a squeeze-stile into the environs of Silsden. Enter Hillcrest Avenue and follow this down to the junction with Skipton Road. Cross and turn right. Now turn first left down the short Briggate and then right down Kirkgate to the Bridge End Inn.

Addingham

The Romans came close to the area which Addingham now occupies. The road that they built between the forts at Ribchester (Bremetennacum), Elslack and Ilkley (Olicana) passed to the south of the town. Indeed, the farm named 'Street' gives indication to the existence and line of an ancient paved road.

Mentioned in the Doomsday Book, Addingham is of Saxon origin – its claim to fame being the fact that Archbishop Wulfere of York fled here to hide from invading Danes in 867 A.D. The village grew from three separate areas, which consisted of Church Street, Old School area and the Green. With the arrival of the industrial revolution, these areas eventually merged into the long ribbon development we see today.

The railway, from Skipton to Ilkley and Leeds, arrived in 1888, the first train running between Colne and Otley. After seventy eight years of operation, final closure came in 1966. The stub of the old embankment can be seen behind the toilets on Main Street. It is hoped that, one day, the Embsay/Bolton Abbey railway will re-open the line back to Addingham.

Addingham Suspension Bridge

In the main street is the arched Lister Barn (dated 1777), which has been used as the Catholic church in the past. Just beyond the barn is The Sailor (1838), originally having a thatched roof. There has been a pub on this site since the 17th century.

As the Heritage Trail leaves Addingham, it crosses the River Wharfe via the suspension bridge,which was built in 1935 to replace an earlier structure, dating from 1895, which was demolished by flood. The river was originally crossed at this location by ferryboat.

Stage 15: Addingham to Bolton Abbey station

Start	Old Station Way GR 077498
Distance	4.5 miles (7.25 km) linear 7.5 miles (12 km) circular
Map	OS Explorer OL21
Parking	Old Station Way

From the junction of Old Station Way and Main Street, cross Main Street into the signed, unmade lane opposite. In 30 metres, turn right to pass through the kissing gate, which sends a tarmac path across the meadow and then over Town Beck via the footbridge. Immediately cross Bolton Road into a delightful, leafy, enclosed way that passes round an old mill pond and emerges into Saw Mill Lane. Follow this to its junction with Ilkley Road. Turn left and, in 100 metres, left again to enter Church Street. At its end, another left turn will send us into North Street (note the Dales Way sign). Cross and advance 200 metres to a second Dales Way sign on the right. Enter this and, in 5 metres, turn right (signed F.P.) to Beamsley. Descend to and cross the suspension bridge spanning the River Wharfe.

Continue ahead on the obvious path and, at its end, turn right through two gates and then left up the access drive from West Hall Farm. At its junction with the lane, continue in the same direction until the lane turns sharp left. Our way is through the gate ahead onto the marked bridleway. Rise up the pastures and pass through two gates to enter a very tightly enclosed bedrock based section. (Hope you don't meet a horse here!) On reaching Low Lathe, the way widens, soon merging onto its access track, which is followed up to Beech House Farm. Pass round the house, then left onto the lane. In 200 metres, turn left at the entrance to Currer Hall. Follow the F.P. sign to Bowers Barn via Howber Hill. Follow the drive, passing the idyllically situated ponds on the right. Just before reaching Farrand House, watch for a step-stile and sign hidden amongst bushes on the right, which sends a slightly discernable path round the left hand side of the field. On passing through a gate, wonderful views are to be seen.

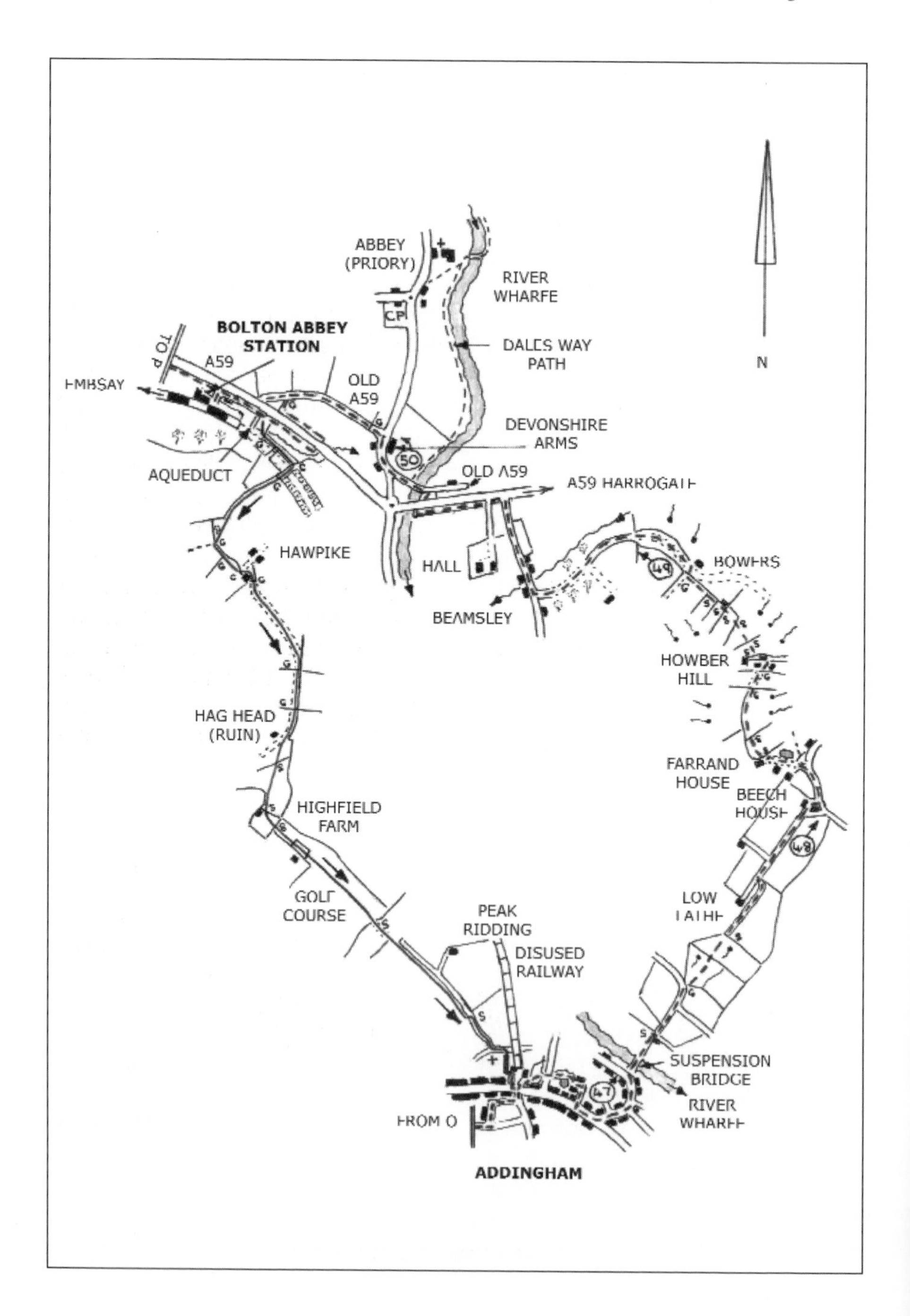
ABBEY
(PRIORY)
CP
RIVER
WHARFE
BOLTON ABBEY
STATION
TO P
DALES WAY
PATH
N
A59
EMBSAY
OLD
A59
DEVONSHIRE
ARMS
50
AQUEDUCT
OLD A59
A59 HARROGATE
HAWPIKE
HALL
BOWERS
49
BEAMSLEY
HOWBER
HILL
HAG HEAD
(RUIN)
FARRAND
HOUSE
BEECH
HOUSE
HIGHFIELD
FARM
48
GOLF
COURSE
LOW
LATHE
PEAK
RIDDING
DISUSED
RAILWAY
SUSPENSION
BRIDGE
47
RIVER
WHARFE
FROM O
ADDINGHAM

Up to the right is Beamsley Beacon, ahead is Simon's Seat and, to its left, Cracoe Rocks on Barden Fell, then Embsay Crag with the two Haws beyond. In the dale bottom are the ruins of Bolton Abbey and, down to the left, our objective – Bolton Abbey station.

Continue ahead, still with the accompanying wall on the left. Pass through a gate/stile in the cross-fence and follow the intake track up to a second gate. Now enclosed, the track passes between the house and barn at Howber Hill to merge with the drive. Do **not** go down the drive, but turn sharp left along a higher drive for 30 metres. Now advance over a step-stile in the wall on the right. Follow the distinct path as it descends Wardla Hill, newly planted with young trees. On reaching Gibbeter Farm, pass to its left and then down the pasture with the wall on the right. At its end, turn right to emerge onto the lane at Bowers Barn. Turn left and pass the cattle-grid. Now follow the quiet lane down to its junction with Beamsley Lane. Turn right, passing through the charming hamlet of Beamsley, to gain the A59. Turn left and, in 50 metres, pass the entrance to Beamsley Hall and enter the path signed Bolton Bridge, which parallels the A59 and passes beneath it on reaching the River Wharfe. Follow the path to the stile, then turn left to cross the Wharfe via the old Bolton Bridge. (Note the Dales Way sign on the right. By following this path along the riverside and back, a detour to Bolton Abbey can be made, extending the route by 1.5 miles.) Advance down the lane (the original A59 before improvements) to its junction with the Grassington road. Turn right to arrive at the Devonshire Arms Hotel and a small traffic island. Cross the road and enter the old disused A59,

Bolton Abbey Station

now a footpath, via a small gate. Follow this for 600 metres, when a sign for Bolton Abbey station sends you left into pastureland. Follow the paved footway to pass beneath the modern A59, after which turn right up to a gateway (note the aqueduct on the left). Pass through the gate to follow the signed path, soon turning left into Bolton Abbey station.

The Return Route

Bolton Abbey station to Addingham

Retrace the Heritage Trail to the gateway at the aqueduct. Turn right alongside the aqueduct to cross the small stone bridge spanning Hambleton Beck. Angle half-left up the pasture to find a gate in the top left hand corner and pass through into an enclosed bridleway, which parallels the disused Ilkley railway line down in the cutting on the right. Ignore the first overbridge and continue to a gate. Turn right to cross the old formation via the second bridge. Now follow the obvious bridleway as it rises with a wall for company on the right. (Note the stone indicating the position of the Borough of Bradford's Waterworks - Nidd aqueduct.) As the climb eases, the bridleway turns half right across to a gate seen ahead. Once through, turn left to pass over Ward Hill. Up to the right is Haw Pike, at 252 metres. Descend gradually towards the environs of Hawpike Farm. Pass to the left of the barn, heading towards the farmhouse, but in 20 metres, turn right onto a fine tractor track. There now follows a fine stride with views down Wharfedale on the left and, ahead, the extensive ridge line of Rombolds Moor, from Nab End down to the Cow and Calf rocks above Ilkley.

On arriving at the remains of Hag Head Laithe, leave the obvious track by turning half-left on a fainter path towards a stone step-stile. Now head towards Highfield Farm, passing to the left of all the buildings, at the end of which pass over the step-stile into a small paddock. Go half-left towards the gate (not the step-stile) which leads onto Addingham's golf course. Follow the green and white marker posts, descending down the course. Leave by a stile to to enter a tree-lined way. Now keeping left at the division of paths, follow the left hand boundary downhill, in tandem with the access drive from Riddings Farm. At the base of this large field, turn left through the gate to gain the drive. Turn right to the junction with Chappel Lane. Turn left, then right into Sugar Hill. On the left is the embankment which carried the old Ilkley railway line. Continue along Sugar Hill, soon arriving at Addingham's main street. Turn left and, in 20 metres, turn right into Old Station Way.

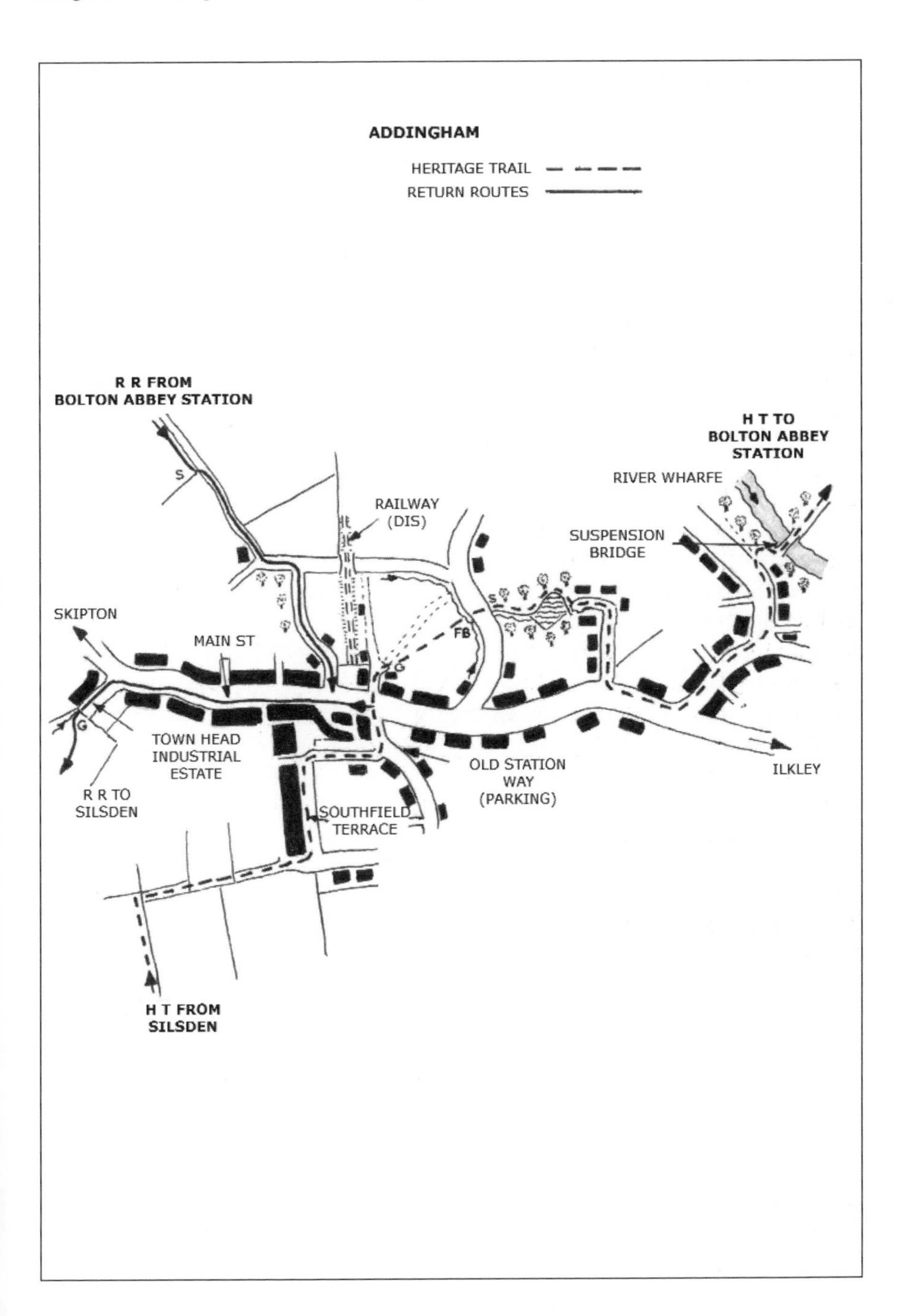
ADDINGHAM
HERITAGE TRAIL
RETURN ROUTES
R R FROM
BOLTON ABBEY STATION
H T TO
BOLTON ABBEY
STATION
RIVER WHARFE
RAILWAY
(DIS)
SUSPENSION
BRIDGE
S
FB
G
SKIPTON
MAIN ST
TOWN HEAD
INDUSTRIAL
ESTATE
R R TO
SILSDEN
SOUTHFIELD
TERRACE
OLD STATION
WAY
(PARKING)
ILKLEY
H T FROM
SILSDEN

Stage 16: Bolton Abbey station – Halton East – Eastby-Embsay station

Start	Bolton Abbey station GR 062534
Distance	3.5 miles (5.6 km) linear 7.5 miles (12 km) circular
Map	OS Explorer OL2
Parking	Bolton Abbey station

Walk down the station's driveway, turning left onto the wide grass verge of the A65. Pass by Hambleton's café and service station and then Hambleton Farm. In 75 metres, cross the A65 to the signed footpath and step-stile opposite, giving access into pastureland. Turn half-left and ascend the large field, gradually distancing yourself from the A65; soon a stone cross-wall will be seen. Locate the step-stile in its top corner and aim for the roof of a building, seen on the skyline, which will lead you to a step-stile in a short section of stone wall. Continue in the same direction to a second short wall with a stile and cross. Ahead now is Fold Barn, dated 1704. Keep to its left and follow its boundary wall round to a gate and advance up the access track into the hamlet of Halton East.

Turn left and walk down through the sleepy hamlet to arrive at a junction. Turn right and, in a few metres, the lane angles right (signed Bolton Abbey) but continue ahead into Moor Lane. Pass a cottage on the left then, in 50 metres, turn left into the access drive to Calm Slate Farm (home of Dales Ice Cream). Pass the house to turn right between the barn and the silage compound. Immediately turn left to attain the stile that gives access to a large meadow. Angle half-right to eventually come alongside the infant Berry Ground Beck and a step-stile in the cross-wall. Now follow the obvious path over two further stiles to reach the access track to Cragg House Farm, which is up to the right. Beyond is High Crag at an elevation of 357 metres.

Cross the access track and angle down right to cross Berry Ground Beck via a stone slab footbridge. Cross the next field diagonally to attain the step-stile which leads onto a tractor track. Follow this unfailingly

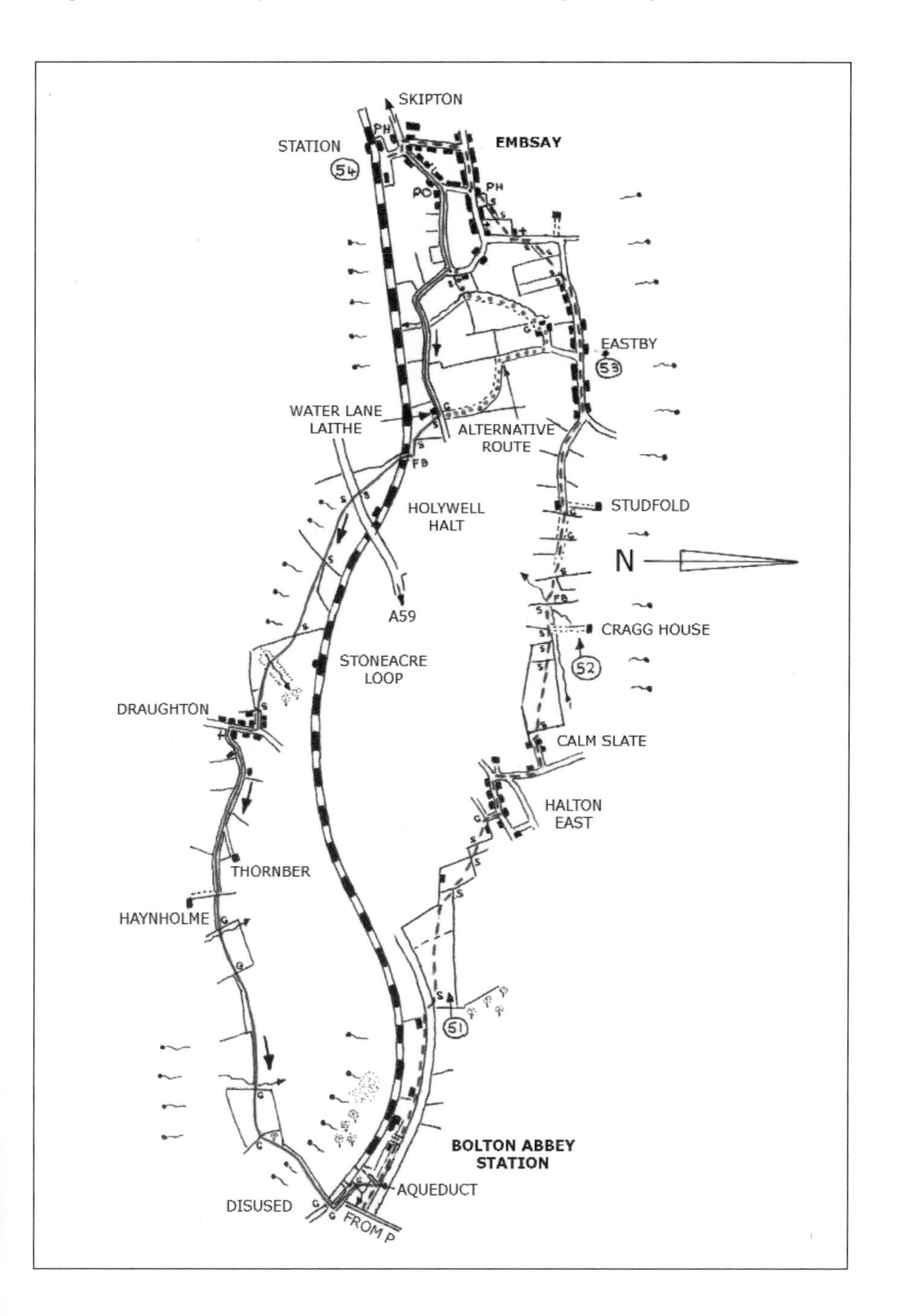
SKIPTON
STATION
54
EMBSAY
PH
PO
PH
EASTBY
53
WATER LANE
LAITHE
ALTERNATIVE
ROUTE
FB
HOLYWELL
HALT
STUDFOLD
N
A59
FB
CRAGG HOUSE
52
STONEACRE
LOOP
DRAUGHTON
CALM SLATE
HALTON
EAST
THORNBER
HAYNHOLME
51
BOLTON ABBEY
STATION
AQUEDUCT
DISUSED
FROM P

through gates to gain Bark Lane at Angrymire Laithe. Now follow the enclosed lane (track) to its end. Turn left and enter the village of Eastby. Continue down the village street (Kirk Lane) passing the Masons Arms on the the left. 50 metres beyond the last house on the left, take the paved path, which leads across two meadows towards Embsay's St. Mary the Virgins church. On reaching the lane, turn left, passing the church lychgate. Shortly, a footpath sign giving access to a meadow will be seen on the right. Cross the meadow to enter a briefly enclosed footway and, at its end, climb the stile. Now angle left down to the car park seen below. Turn right onto the road to gain the Elm Tree Inn at Embsay's Elm Tree Square. Continue ahead into Pasture Road, which is followed to the junction with West Lane. Turn left and descend West Lane to its end and junction with East Lane. Directly across is the Cavendish Arms, turn left up East Lane and then immediately right into the access drive into Embsay station.

Cavendish Arms

The Return Route

Embsay station – Draughton – Bolton Abbey station

The final leg of the Heritage Trail begins at the entrance to Embsay station. Turn right and ascend East Lane for 400 metres, turning right again into Shires Lane with the post office on the right. Pass the immaculate cricket club and turn right at the junction onto Low Lane, signed Halton East. (To avoid more road walking, an alternative route turns left for 50 metres and takes the footpath on the right, which follows Rowton Beck up to Rowton Farm, turning right on to the bridleway down to Water Lane Laithe - see map.)

Follow Low Lane to Water Lane Laithe, with views of the Embsay and Bolton Abbey railway on the right and, beyond, the Skibedon quarry rockface. Pass over the stile just beyond the Laithe to go diagonally left across the meadow, to find the stile adjacent to the railway. Parallel the line up to the footbridge and cross. Now rise up the field, gradually distancing yourself from the right-hand boundary, to find the stile onto the A65. Go directly across and follow the sign directing you across a massive field. Aim for a stone wall going away, seen in the distance. Go over the rise and descend to a step-stile in a cross-wall. Now the wall mentioned earlier will be on your left. This is followed until it turns left. Continue ahead, aiming for a stile seen up on the skyline. From here, the passing loop and signal box at Stoneacre can be seen down to the left. The route of the railway can be traced down the valley of Ings Beck, almost as far as Bolton Abbey station. From the stile, continue half-right in the direction of a large barn, which is not reached. After 200 metres, the route delves into a small clough to cross a small beck via a stone footbridge. Rise up the bank and continue towards the corner of a stone wall that will be seen ahead. Advance in the same direction to find the step-stile leading into the drive at Draughton Hall Farm. Pass down the drive and, on reaching the road, turn right into the idyllic village of Draughton. Pass the hall on the right to arrive at the old school house and the tiny church dedicated to St. Augustine on the left, the foundation stone of which was laid by the Duchess of Devonshire on 23rd August 1897.

Turn left to pass between school, village hall and church to follow the surfaced, enclosed bridleway, keeping right at the first junction, shortly after which it becomes unsurfaced and descends to a gate. On the right is Haynholme Farm, with a glimpse of wind turbines on Chelker Hill beyond. Pass through the gate into pastureland and with a wall for

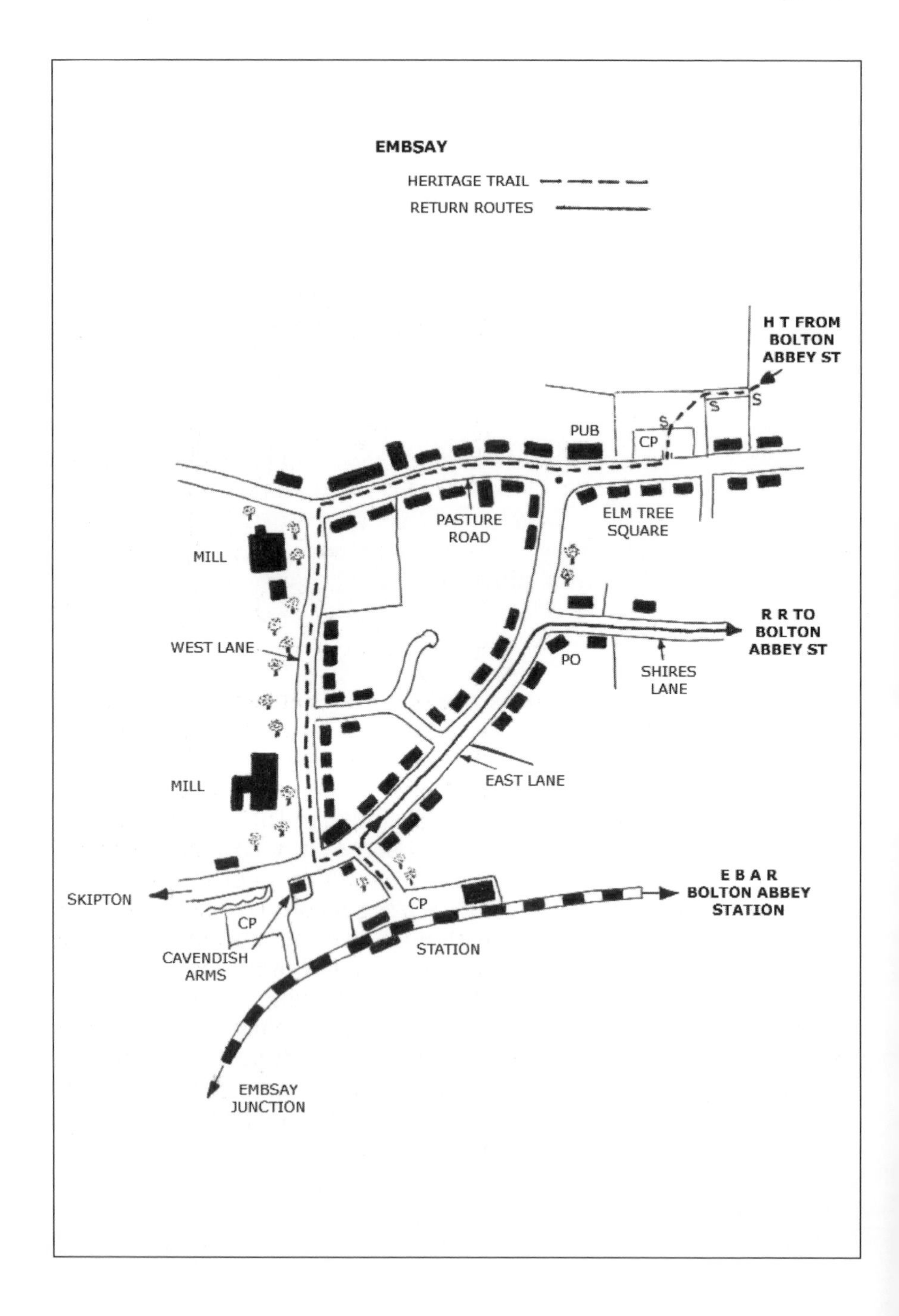
EMBSAY
HERITAGE TRAIL
RETURN ROUTES
H T FROM
BOLTON
ABBEY ST
S
S
S
PUB
CP
PASTURE
ROAD
ELM TREE
SQUARE
MILL
R R TO
BOLTON
ABBEY ST
WEST LANE
PO
SHIRES
LANE
MILL
EAST LANE
SKIPTON
CP
CP
CAVENDISH
ARMS
STATION
E B A R
BOLTON ABBEY
STATION
EMBSAY
JUNCTION

St. Augustine Draughton

company on the right, descend to the slab-bridge at Banks Gill Beck. Our way is now straight forward and, although pathless, simply pass over the rise to find a gate in the cross-wall. Now accompany the wall on the right down to the gate at Harry Wall Gill. Cross the next pasture, with Haw Pike up to the right, and pass through the gate at Ward Hill. Ahead, there are fine views down into Wharfedale and Bolton Abbey, with Simons Seat and Beamsley Beacon forming the perfect backdrop, whilst, on the left, glimpses of Bolton Abbey station can be seen. Follow the now well defined green bridleway as it descends with a wall on the left (note the stone marking the line of Bradford Corporation's water works - Nidd aqueduct). Advance through a gate and cross the bridge spanning the disused Bolton Abbey/Addingham railway line. At its far end, immediately turn left into the enclosed bridleway, with the old line in the cutting on the left. Pass by a second overbridge and then through a small gate. Now angle right and descend to cross Hambleton Beck, with the aqueduct on the left. Continue up to the gate, then follow the signed path to Bolton Abbey station.

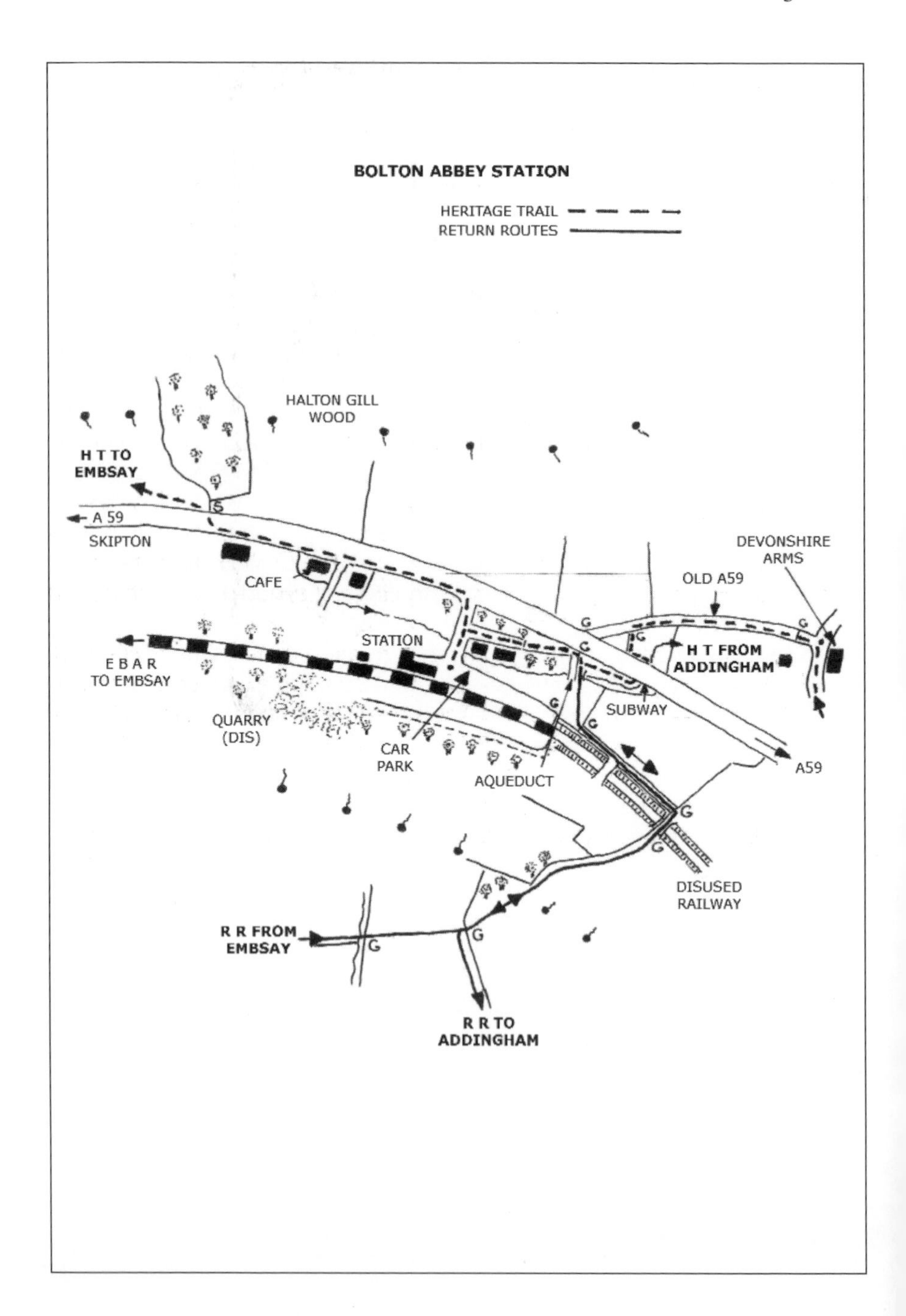
BOLTON ABBEY STATION
HERITAGE TRAIL
RETURN ROUTES
HALTON GILL WOOD
H T TO EMBSAY
A 59
SKIPTON
CAFE
STATION
E B A R TO EMBSAY
QUARRY (DIS)
CAR PARK
AQUEDUCT
SUBWAY
DEVONSHIRE ARMS
OLD A59
H T FROM ADDINGHAM
A59
DISUSED RAILWAY
R R FROM EMBSAY
R R TO ADDINGHAM

Embsay and Bolton Abbey Steam Railway

In July, 1883, a bill was passed through parliament to build a double-track line of almost 12 miles from Skipton to Ilkley via Embsay, Bolton Abbey and Addingham. Work started in 1885, and the first train completed the journey, from Colne to Otley, on 1 October, 1888.

The route remained open for 77 years before closure on 5 July, 1965. Three years later, a group of enthusiasts formed the Embsay and Grassington Preservation Society, their objective being to re-open the branch to Grassington, which was scheduled to close. However, with the boom in motorway construction, the branch was reprieved for the conveyance of road stone from Swindon quarry. The Society then had to look elsewhere, and in 1970, a lease was obtained from British Rail for the site at Embsay station. The group then became the Yorkshire Dales Railway Museum Trust. There then followed a period of consolidation, acquiring locos and stock during the period of renovation, and there were also limited train rides.

In May 1979, the official re-opening was performed by the Bishop of Bradford. Skibden was the terminus until 1986, when the line was extended to Holywell Halt, where a platform and picnic area have been constructed. In 1992, a further extension followed to Stoneacre passing loop, equipped with a brick and timber signal box. After another five years dedication and hard work, the volunteers reached Bolton Abbey station, which extended the line to 4.5 miles. The station at Bolton Abbey was newly constructed in 1994, and is a replica of the original, which fell into decay during its thirty-two year closure.

Bolton Abbey Priory

Thousands of tourists visit the Priory every year to enjoy its idyllic setting between the River Wharfe and wooded hillsides. Originally founded at Embsay, in 1120, by Cecily de Romilly, of Skipton castle, and William Meschine, it was later transferred to Bolton in 1154. The ruins seen today date mainly from the 14th century, the exception being the hall, which was constructed in the 16th century.

When visiting the Priory, a walk along the Strid Wood Nature Trail should be made, which is gained by the small kiosk at the Cavendish Pavilion car park, where a small guide book will be available. The climax of the walk is the Strid, where the River Wharfe is funnelled through a narrow rock chasm, the currents of which have claimed many lives over the years.

Bolton Abbey Priory